Lewis & Clark's
Northwest
Journey

"Weather Disagreeable!"

by George R. Miller

Frank
Amato
PORTLAND

All inquiries should be addressed to:
Frank Amato Publications, Inc.
P.O. Box 82112 • Portland, Oregon 97282
503-653-8108 • www.amatobooks.com

Book Design: Amy Tomlinson
All photos and illustrations by George R. Miller, unless otherwise noted.
Cover illustration by Loren Smith.

Softbound ISBN: 1-57188-323-1
Softbound UPC: 0-81127-00157-6

Printed in Hong Kong
1 3 5 7 8 10 8 6 4 2

TABLE OF CONTENTS

Introduction 7

Chapter 1:
From the Rocky Mountains to the Pacific Ocean 8
*Early September snowstorms; thunderstorms; canyon winds; beautiful fall weather;
wind and rain.*

Chapter 2:
Along the Pacific Coast 20
*Rain, rain, and more rain; storminess; lightning, thunder and hail;
freezing weather for two weeks; a touch of spring.*

Chapter 3:
From the Pacific Ocean to the Rocky Mountains 43
Gusty winds; more rain; warm temperatures; high water; deep snow.

Epilogue 70

Bibliography 72

Glossary 74

Index 76

Dedication

*This book is dedicated to my wife Janice and to everyone who has enjoyed
the journals of the Lewis and Clark Expedition.*

Acknowledgments

Many individuals helped in the construction and proofreading of this manuscript. My wife, Janice, once again tirelessly read and re-read the manuscript. David Olsen, retired Area Manager for the National Weather Service of Montana, now living in Battle Ground, Washington, provided many helpful suggestions as did Dr. Dan Johnson, Geography Department, Portland State University, and Mark Nelsen, Chief Meteorologist for KPTV in Portland, Oregon. John Jannuzzi, Meteorologist in Charge of the National Weather Service Forecast Office in Boise, Idaho offered excellent advice regarding the Idaho portion. Charles Orwig, former Hydrologist in Charge, Portland, Oregon River Forecast Center, National Weather Service, gave expert advice regarding river levels and heights. Francine Kirsch, author and freelance writer, provided initial suggestions regarding publisher contacts. The journals edited by Gary Moulton were invaluable regarding precise locations of where the Corps of Discovery camped. Kim Koch at Frank Amato Publications again provided expert editorial advice. Amy Tomlinson, freelance designer, did the wonderful layout and design work. To all of the above, you were certainly not "disagreeable," but extremely helpful.

Foreword

Their clothes were rotting due to the dampness. Their meat was spoiling due to the warmth. Wind and waves prevented them from exploring. Many entries in the Corps of Discovery logbooks from the Rocky Mountains to the Pacific Ocean and back to the Rockies contain the term, "The weather is disagreeable!" But was it always that bad? Was the weather the Corps of Discovery experienced from the Rocky Mountains to the Pacific Ocean 1805-1806 different from the weather today?

An early fall snowstorm greeted the party as they crossed the Rocky Mountains. While constructing their canoes at Canoe Camp on the Clearwater River, and for a period before and after, they experienced some warm, dry, beautiful fall weather. Brief rain greeted the party as they descended the Columbia River. Strong Pacific wind and rainstorms buffeted and drenched them while camped at the mouth of the Columbia River.

A cold arctic outbreak that lasted for two weeks deposited six inches or more of snow on their camp at Fort Clatsop and icicles hung from the eaves. Their return up the Columbia River was interrupted by strong east winds and then strong west winds through the Columbia River Gorge. Deep winter snow delayed their safe journey across the Rocky Mountains.

Members of the Corps of Discovery battled snow while crossing the Rocky Mountains in September 1805 and again in June 1806. Snow lay on the ground for two weeks at Fort Clatsop on the Pacific Ocean while the party was camped there.

The forecast for tomorrow's weather captures our attention on a daily basis. What we wear, where we go, what we eat are all weather dependent. So it was also with the Corps of Discovery, but they had no forecast to rely on. Their daily events were often interrupted by weather conditions. Were those conditions different from the ones that disrupt our daily activities today?

Members of the Lewis and Clark Expedition took meticulous observations regarding weather conditions, often several times a day. This book looks at those notations and compares them with weather conditions today, from the Rocky Mountains to the Pacific Ocean. It then speculates as to the weather patterns the Corps of Discovery may have experienced.

Accurate weather observations go back about 250 years in the United States from locations near the eastern seaboard. In the western portion of the country, the period is much less. Systematic observations began at Astoria, Oregon in the mid-1850s and the mid-1870s from Walla Walla, Washington and The Dalles, Oregon and Portland, Oregon. Those stations are along the trail the Corps of Discovery followed. Has the weather at those locations changed?

A storm entering California provides a brief respite from the rain in northwest Oregon. However, a stronger storm to the west is rapidly approaching the coast, bringing more rain.

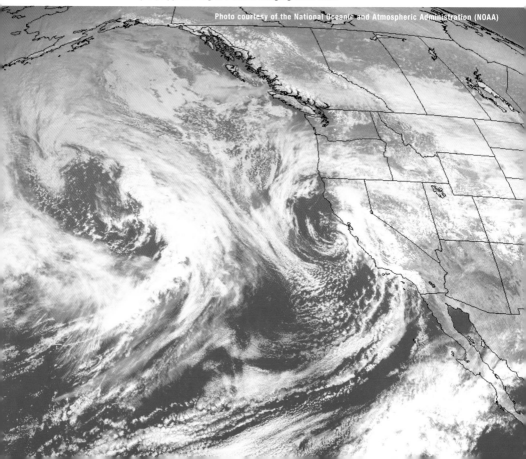

Introduction

In reading the journals of the Corps of Discovery, this author was amazed at the many notations regarding the weather. Not only did Meriwether Lewis and William Clark keep meticulous weather notations, but other members of the Corps of Discovery did also. All of these entries are examined in detail in this book and comparisons are made. Occasionally, there are discrepancies, but for the most part each daily entry is compatible with the other.

Some controversy surrounds the issue of just when the entries were made. Was it on that exact day? Was it from memory a few days later? Was it in discussion with other members of the team? These questions will never be fully answered. But the fact remains: the Corps of Discovery followed President Thomas Jefferson's instructions to record the weather of this yet unexplored area.

At the end of each month the Captains entered their observations in a coded form: "f" for fair; "r" for rain, "s" for snow; "h" for hail; "t" for thunder; "l" for lightning; "c" for cloudy. Thus, an entry such as: "c.a.r.," would mean that it was cloudy after rain. There is no code for sunny or clear and the author believes that many of those entries listed as "fair" were meant to indicate sunny or even partly sunny conditions. Most observations by the Captains were taken at sunrise and at 4 p.m., and the reader should remember that the hour of sunrise varied considerably during the time they were on their mission. Times are generally not noted in weather references by other members of the party.

Then, as now, weather is a fascinating topic. Weather occurrences prevent or interrupt us from doing our daily planned activities. So it was with the Corps of Discovery.

✳ ✳ ✳

"Your observations are to be taken with great pains & accuracy..."
"Other objects worthy of notice will be...Climate, as character-
ized by the thermometer, by the proportion of rainy, cloudy, and clear
days, by lightning, hail, snow, ice, by the access and recess of frost, by the
winds prevailing at different seasons..."

Jefferson's Instructions to Lewis. 20 June 1803.

Chapter**One**

From the Rocky Mountains
to the Pacific Ocean

September 15 to November 15, 1805

After a bitterly cold winter (1804-1805) with the Mandans in what is now North Dakota, the Corps of Discovery proceeded west to cross the Rocky Mountains. The weather in 1804 could very well have been linked to a strong El Niño episode in 1803-1804.[1] El Niño occurrences are often related to a displacement of the jet stream, that "river of air" 4 to 8 miles above sea level, northward into Canada and Alaska and thence southeastward into the middle portion of the United States. This may have been the cause of the very cold winter the Corps of Discovery experienced at Fort Mandan.

On September 13, 1805, the Corps of Discovery crossed what is now the Idaho-Montana state line into Idaho. They were traveling the Lolo Trail, a route Native Americans had used for years to cross the north-central Idaho and western Montana mountains. Fall was rapidly approaching and earlier storms had left snow on the higher peaks. Weather had often been a factor in their journey so far. It would continue to be.

※   ※   ※

"I have been wet and as cold in every part as I ever was in my life, indeed I was at one time fearfull my feet would freeze in the thin mockersons which I wore..."

William Clark, September 16, 1805,
perhaps on Moon Creek, Idaho County, Idaho.
The Journals of the Lewis & Clark Expedition, Volume 5,
Gary E. Moulton, Editor

Snow in the north-central Idaho mountains in mid-September is not an unusual occurrence. Indeed, snow has been recorded much earlier at even lower elevations in northwestern Montana and northern Idaho. The explorers

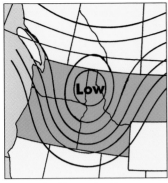

Fig. 1.1 A cold upper-level low-pressure area moving through the north-central Idaho Rocky Mountains can bring snow in early fall.

likely encountered a slow-moving trough of low pressure in the middle and upper levels of the atmosphere (10,000 to 40,000 feet) with its attendant cold air. (See Figure 1.1) Lolo Pass is at an elevation of 5,233 feet and the Lolo Trail they were following is between 5,000 and 6,000 feet in elevation. They remark, "...a Bank of old Snow about 3 feet deep lying on the Northern Side of the <hills> mountain and in Small banks on the top & leavel parts of the mountain..." The snow may have been deposited from an earlier storm in September.

The weather during their journey became much more agreeable after the early fall snowstorm. Other than a thunder-shower on the 24th of September, the group enjoyed a long stretch of warm, fall weather that lasted through almost the entire month of October.

✳   ✳   ✳

"A hard wind and rain at dark. hot day. at dark a hard wind from The S W accompaned with rain which lasted half an hour."

William Clark, September 23, 1805,
about a mile southwest of Weippe, Clearwater County, Idaho.
The Journals of the Lewis & Clark Expedition, Volume 5,
Gary E. Moulton, Editor

Clark's entry for sunrise on September 24 begins with: "fair after rain and thunder and lightning." Late summer and early fall thunder-storms over the mountains of central Idaho normally result from a northward movement of warm moist tropical air from the Gulf of Mexico or the Gulf of California. These storms are gen-erally preceded by hot surface temperatures. Such seems to have been the case during this period in mid-September 1805. Clark's entry for September 21st indicates, "The day proved warm," and on the 22nd, "a verry worm day."

Thunderstorms are the result of an atmos-phere that in meteorological terms is called "unstable." Air that is heated at the surface by

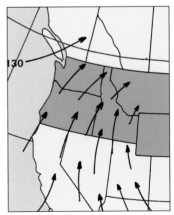

Fig. 1.2 Very warm surface tempera-tures combined with warm, moist southerly winds aloft (arrows) can create thunderstorms over the north-central Idaho Rocky Mountains.

solar radiation rises. If that air is warmer than air it comes in contact with as it rises, it will continue to rise. Adding moisture to the ascending column of air makes it even more unstable. Such was the likely scenario for this strong thunderstorm experienced by the Corps of Discovery on the Clearwater River near Orofino, Idaho. (See Figure 1.2)

The thundershower appears to have been only a short break from the warmth of late September experienced by the party well into October. Patrick Gass's entry for September 25, 1805 states, "The climate here is warm; and the heat to day was as great as we had experienced at any time during the summer."

✳ ✳ ✳

"The easterly winds which blow imediately off the mountains are very cool untill 10 a.m. when the day becomes verry warm and the winds Shift about."

William Clark, October 3, 1805,
on the Clearwater River west of Orofino, Idaho.
The Journals of the Lewis & Clark Expedition, Volume 5,
Gary E. Moulton, Editor

From September 26 through October 6, 1805, the Corps of Discovery remained on the Clearwater River at a place called Canoe Camp roughly five miles west of the town of Orofino, Idaho. The Clearwater River canyon at this point is oriented almost due east-west. It is an excellent location to experience upcanyon and downcanyon winds. William Clark's keen meteorological observation makes note of this.

Fig. 1.3 Cool downcanyon winds from an easterly direction occur frequently along the Clearwater River in Idaho from late-night to early morning hours under clear skies.

After the sun has set on the higher elevations around the canyon, the air here begins to cool, losing its heat to radiation. The cooler air, since it is slightly more dense, begins a slow journey down the slopes into the bottom of the canyon. This process continues throughout the night as the earth loses more heat to space via radiation. Downcanyon winds increase during the night and reach their peak around sunrise and begin decreasing. (See Figure 1.3)

After sunrise, radiation from the sun begins warming the hills surrounding the valley. This air is heated by being in contact with the earth and begins to rise, moving up the slopes on either side of the canyon. As air molecules

Fig. 1.4 Warm upcanyon winds from a westerly direction occur frequently along the Clearwater River in Idaho. As the air is heated, it begins to rise during late-morning hours, then reaches peak speed in late afternoon.

leave one area, other air molecules move in to take their place; in this case, from lower down in the canyon. As the day progresses, continued warming of the air causes it to begin moving up the canyon, slowly at first and then stronger as the day progresses. (See Figure 1.4)

On only a few days while camped at Canoe Camp are the above conditions disrupted. Wind flows from high pressure into an area of lower pressure. Small disturbances in the general wind flow can cause these variations or disruptions. Often, they can increase or decrease the upcanyon and downcanyon breezes. Cloud cover can cause a decrease in canyon winds since clouds prevent the earth's radiation from escaping into space at night and limiting the sun's radiation from reaching the earth during the day. Upcanyon and downcanyon winds occur with regularity today in canyons everywhere.

✳ ✳ ✳

"a windey dark raney morning The rain commenced before day and continued moderately untill near 12 oClock."

William Clark, October 13, 1805,
along the Snake River near Ayer, Washington.
The Journals of the Lewis & Clark Expedition, Volume 5,
Gary E. Moulton, Editor

By mid-October the jet stream, that quite likely had remained north of the Pacific Northwest throughout the summer and early fall, now shows signs of moving south. The rain on the 13th of October was preceded by strong south to southwesterly winds as an early fall storm front was approaching the area. (Figure 1.5) These winds are not uncommon over southeastern Washington along the Snake River and they can be enhanced as storm systems move across southern Canada. Local terrain can cause wide variations in speed and direction. Even post frontal conditions, where the Pacific high-pressure area is expanding into

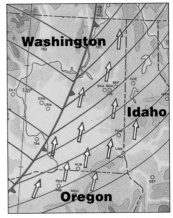

Fig. 1.5 Strong south to southwesterly winds can occur ahead of a cold front as it moves across eastern Washington.

the Pacific Northwest, cause a strong pressure gradient to develop with strong west to southwest winds as the result. (See Figure 1.6)

After this brief rainstorm, however, the Corps of Discovery once again experienced the last of a fine, clear period of fall weather until late October. From October 20 to November 2, 1805 the Corps of Discovery passed through the Columbia River Gorge. This stretch of geography of roughly 100 miles has one of the most distinct climate changes found anywhere, certainly within the United States. Throughout the eastern portion of this path that the Columbia River takes through the Cascade Mountains, from near Arlington, Oregon to The Dalles, Oregon, the annual precipitation is around 10 inches.

Fig. 1.6 As the cold front moves across eastern Washington, surface winds shift to a more westerly direction. A strong pressure gradient can even increase the wind speed.

✳ ✳ ✳

"Rained all the evening & blew hard from the West.
Here the mountains are high on each Side, the high points
of those to the Lard. has Snow."

William Clark, October 28, 1805,
while camped near The Dalles, Oregon.
The Journals of the Lewis & Clark Expedition, Volume 5,
Gary E. Moulton, Editor

William Clark's entry for October 20, 1805 while camped near Roosevelt, Klickitat County, Washington was, "The Star Side is high rugid hills, the Lard. side a low plain and **not a tree to be Seen in any direction** (author's emphasis) except a fiew Small willow bushes which are Scattered partially on the Sides of the bank." The country is barren, (Figure 1.7), and the scant amount of annual precipitation supports only sage and scrub brush. Indeed, in their travels both up and down the river, the party sometimes had to trade for firewood to cook their meals or go completely without.

Traveling down the Columbia River, vegetation begins to increase near The Dalles, Oregon. Joseph Whitehouse, in his journal for October 25, 1805, writes, "The hills the whole of this distance, were high on both sides of the River, and we saw some pine & Oak timber." From October 25-27 the party was camped at the mouth of Mill Creek near The Dalles.

As one travels westward from The Dalles, annual precipitation increases to

Fig. 1.7 The hills of eastern Oregon as shown from the Washington side of the Columbia River are mostly bare of vegetation. The Corps of Discovery camped near here on October 20, 1805 on their trip down river.

around 30 inches at Hood River, Oregon. Clark writes on October 28 while slightly west of The Dalles, "The Countrey begin to be thinly timbered with Pine & low white oake verry rocky and hilley." Figure 1.8 shows the area just west of The Dalles, Oregon. On October 29, as the party passed through what is now the Hood River/White Salmon area, John Ordway entered in his journal, "the country Mountaineous. high clifts on the River. Mostly covred with pine timber. Some cotten wood on the narrow bottoms. some willow also." This dramatic change of climate from dry at the east end to wet at the west end has existed for thousands of years, increasing as the Cascade Mountains grew, sapping moisture out of a prevailing flow of westerly air aloft.

The party is also beginning to notice that snow has fallen over the higher peaks and mountains. The storm they encountered on October 13, 1805 could

Fig. 1.8 Vegetation through the Columbia River Gorge begins increasing west of The Dalles, Oregon. The party camped just east of this location on October 28, 1805.

very likely have been accompanied by air cool enough aloft to have lowered the freezing level to around 5,000 feet.

But it is the wind that the party remarks on frequently, and often they were detained by waves on the river created by a strong west wind. Clark writes on October 28, 1805 about the natives, "The wind which is the cause of our delay, does not retard the motions of those people at all, as their canoes are calculated to ride the highest waves..." and Whitehouse writes on the same day, "We continued on our way a short distance further down the River, when the Wind rose so high from the Westward, & the Waves ran also so high, that our officers thought it dangerous to proceed."

Conifer trees exposed to the wind in the eastern portion of the Columbia River Gorge

Fig. 1.9 Strong westerly winds from early spring to mid-fall at the eastern end of the Columbia River Gorge prevent much foliage from growing on the west side of trees.

have virtually no branches on their western sides (Figure 1.9). This is due to the prevailing westerly wind in the Gorge from April through October. This wind is the result of a large pressure difference between the Pacific Ocean to the west where higher pressure is located and lower pressure east of the Cascade Mountains. (See Figure 1.10) The wind was troublesome for the Corps of Discovery but today the area is a haven for windsurfers. These winds begin decreasing in intensity during October, but their persistent presence throughout October 1805 suggests that the Pacific high-pressure area offshore was reluctant to begin its annual migration southward.

But by late October 1805 it was losing the battle with a jet stream that was slowly migrating south. It began to rain on October 28 and Clark notes on October 31, 1805, "A Cloudy rainey disagreeable morning." In early November, however, as the Corps of Discovery progressed through the western portion of the Columbia River Gorge, they were granted a reprieve from the rain.

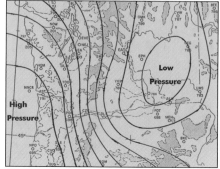

Fig. 1.10 Surface high pressure offshore and surface low pressure over eastern Washington create a strong pressure gradient through the Columbia River Gorge from April to October. (Lines are isobars, or lines of equal pressure.)

Sunny, warm, fall days are often reluctant to leave completely. Frequently after two or three early fall storms, the Pacific high-pressure area offshore will rebound and provide Pacific Northwest residents with clear, crisp Indian Summer weather.[2] This often-rapid building of high pressure over Washington and Oregon will produce a northeast wind with its accompanied fair weather. Clark writes on November 1, 1805 near what is now Bonneville Dam, "a verry cold morning wind from N.E. and hard." This stretch of beautiful fall weather continued for four days. By November 2, 1805, however, the easterly wind had ceased.

The earlier series of fall storms that brought rain to the region would have dampened the ground. The Corps of Discovery had no weather forecast on November 2, 1805, but with clear skies, light winds and sufficient soil moisture, the forecast would have been for fog on the morning of the 3rd. Clark writes on November 3, 1805, at their camp near Rooster Rock State Park, Multnomah County, "The Fog So thick this morning that we could not See a man 50 Steps off, this fog detained us untill 10 oClock at which time we Set out." The fog lifted around noon, into low stratus clouds, and the weather cleared. It was the last warm, completely sunny day the party would experience for some time. On November 4, 1805 it became cloudy and began to rain.

Weather-reporting stations in the Pacific Northwest show a marked increase from October amounts of precipitation to those in November, often twice as much. At Portland, Oregon the average monthly precipitation for October is 2.67 inches. That increases to 5.34 in November. At Astoria, Oregon where the Corps of Discovery would spend the winter, October average precipitation is 5.73 inches, increasing to 10.05 in November. The party was on the verge of experiencing a cool, damp Pacific Northwest winter.

✳ ✳ ✳

"we are all wet Cold and disagreeable, rain Continues & encreases."

William Clark, November 5, 1805,
near the mouth of the Kalama River, Washington.
The Journals of the Lewis & Clark Expedition, Volume 6
Gary E. Moulton, Editor.

Hills press close to the Columbia River between Woodland and Kalama, Washington. The author travels this road frequently and either observes the wind blowing from a south-southeasterly direction or a north-northwesterly direction depending on the season of the year. It is rarely calm. Clark's notation on November 5, 1805 was, "The high Hills which run in a N.W. & S.E. derection form both banks of the river the Shore boald and rockey, the hills rise gradually & are Covered with a thick groth of pine &c." But in this area it was not the wind that was bothersome, it was the rain.

It seems evident that a strong west-southwesterly jet stream had indeed become established over the Pacific Northwest. (Figure 1.11) Rain was entered in the journals every day as the party passed the mouth of the Cowlitz River on November 6, 1805 and Cathlamet and Skamakowa, Washington

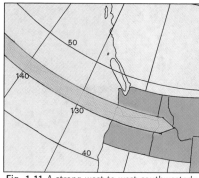

Fig. 1.11 A strong west to west-southwesterly jet stream into the Pacific Northwest brings frequent storms into the area.

on the 7th. On the morning of November 8, the party received a brief respite from the rain camped near Grays Bay and perhaps even some filtered sunlight shining through a heavy blanket of cirrostratus clouds. Patrick Gass's entry for that day indicates, "The morning was cloudy and there was a hard wind from the east." The party was no doubt between storms.

Easterly winds with cloudy conditions near the mouth of the Columbia

Fig. 1.12 Strong south-southwesterly winds blowing across the open water of the Columbia River would create large waves crashing against the party's November 8 & 9, 1805 campsite.

River in late fall, winter and early spring generally mean that another storm system is approaching as air flows from higher pressure inland to lower pressure off the coast. These winds can cause high swells on the river. By afternoon the rain had commenced once again, and the wind had shifted to a more southerly direction and was increasing.

The Columbia River near the Pacific/Wahkiakum County line in Washington is from six to ten miles wide. This is a long enough fetch for high waves to form, especially with a strong southerly wind. (Figure 1.12) Clark's entry for November 8, 1805 indicates, "The Seas roled and tossed the Canoes in such a manner this evening that several of our party were Sea Sick." They were pinned down on the north shore of the Columbia River.

November 9 brought no relief from the rain. A shift in the wind to a more southwesterly direction, however, could suggest the brunt of the storm was passing. Clark's entry on November 9 states, "at 4 oClock the wind Shifted about to

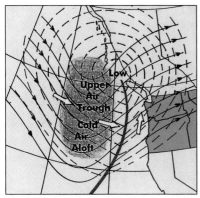

Fig. 1.13 A Pacific storm front approaching the coast followed by a trough of low pressure aloft with colder air. (Surface isobars are dashed lines and upper air flow solid lines.)

the S.W imediately from the ocian and blew a Storm for about 2 hours." Was the strong Pacific storm front about to pass?

Storm fronts moving onshore in the Pacific Northwest from the Pacific Ocean are generally preceded by strong southerly winds. As the front passes the winds show a clockwise shift in direction and in most cases a decrease in speed. Precipitation often becomes showery or ceases for a period of time. Such was the entry by Joseph Whitehouse on November 9, "it ceased raining in the evening." But the break in the rain was very brief. Clark notes on the morning of November 10, "rained verry hard the greater part of the last night & Continus this morning, the wind has layed and the Swells are fallen." But how long would the lull in the storm and wind continue? There is some suggestion that perhaps the break was quite brief.

A cold upper-level trough of low pressure accompanies every storm front that enters the Pacific Northwest from the ocean. (Figure 1.13) Often, these perturbations in the jet stream move slowly eastward through the area. Winds gradually shift to the northwest at all levels of the atmosphere occurring first at the surface. As the party canoed along the north shore of the Columbia River approaching Point Ellice, they would have been sheltered from a northwesterly wind.[3]

The orientation of the Columbia River from Point Ellice to the ocean is northwesterly. This offers a long fetch for a northwesterly wind to create huge swells. (Figure 1.14) Such was the situation that greeted the party as they tried to move around the point from perhaps relatively weaker winds and smaller waves. Once again they had to turn around and head back. The ocean was close, but very treacherous conditions prevailed over these last few miles.

Fig. 1.14 Strong northwesterly winds at the mouth of the Columbia River can create large waves over this stretch of the river that would decrease east of Point Ellice as the winds in this area decrease.

Often a shift in the wind from southerly to a more northwesterly direction signals clearing skies. On the Pacific Northwest coast, however, when a series of storms one right after the other buffets the area, there is often little time for clearing. Cloudiness and precipitation from the next storm begin affecting the area.[4] There is no break in the rain, and the wind gradually shifts around to a more southerly or southwesterly direction.

When there is a very short break between storms, or literally no break, continuous rain begins to saturate the soils. They are loosened and begin to slide. Clark writes on November 11, 1805, "the great quantites of rain which has loosened the Stones on the hill Sides, and the Small Stones fall down upon us." The cold, wet party could go nowhere on this date, and little did they know that they would soon be visited by another cold upper-level trough during the early morning hours of November 12, 1805. The jet stream appears to be shifting slightly to a more west-northwesterly orientation.

* * *

"a hard Storm continued all last night, and hard Thunder lightning and hail this morning. we Saw a mountain on the opposite Shore covred with Snow."

John Ordway, November 12, 1805,
camped near Point Ellice on north side of Columbia River.
The Journals of the Lewis & Clark Expedition Volume 9,
Gary E. Moulton, Editor.

With a strong jet stream oriented from the west-northwest to the east-southeast (Figure 1.15), upper-level troughs moving along this corridor are capable of lowering the freezing level of the free air to values as low as 2,000 to 2,500 feet. The intrusion of cold air aloft creates an atmosphere that is unstable, just the right condition for thunderstorms to develop that often bring with them small hail or ice pellets. Higher elevations begin to show white.

Saddle Mountain is a little over 20 miles south-southeast of where the Corps of Discovery was camped November 10-14, 1805. It rises to an elevation of 3,283 feet and is easily visible from the north shore of the Columbia River. (Figure 1.16) The top of it is frequently covered with snow in the winter. The clouds have lifted enough

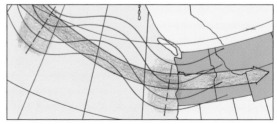

Fig. 1.15 A strong west-northwesterly jet stream can bring a series of cold upper-level troughs into the Pacific Northwest with little break in between storms.

for the party to view it, and Clark makes mention of this with the remark, "...it then became light for a short time when the heavens became darkined by a black Cloud from the S,W, & a hard rain. . . It was clear at 12 for a Short time. I observed the Mountains on the opposite Side was

Fig. 1.16 Saddle Mountain in Oregon, elevation 3,283 feet, is clearly visible from the north side of the Columbia River. Photo was taken near where the Corps of Discovery camped November 10-14, 1805.

covered with Snow." Captain Lewis, in his weather table for November 12, writes, "Cleared off a Short time & raind until 12 oClock Cleared off a hour and rainrd again." Had there been a weather forecast, it would probably have been: Showers and an occasional thundershower with brief clearing periods.

True wind direction is hard to determine in a dense forest or behind hills. On November 13, Captain Clark climbs the steep hill in back of their camp. When he reaches the top which is near 1,000 feet, he discovers that the wind is, "high from the N.W. and waves high at a Short distance below our Encampment." The hail of yesterday remained on the ground indicating that the temperatures must have been around 40°F, but with a strong wind, it must have felt like it was in the 30s. Wind chill contributed to their plight.[5]

Once again this fits well with the passage of an upper-level trough; northwesterly winds that the party would not have noticed in the trees at their campsite, but which were very capable of generating waves on the Columbia. Temperatures would have been quite cool. The rain continued throughout most of November 14, 1805, but on November 15, the party was greeted with their first taste of fair weather during the last ten days. But would it continue?

1. Quinn, William H., Climatic Variations in Southern California Over the Past 2000 Years Based on the El Niño/Southern Oscillation, College of Oceanography, Oregon State University, Corvallis, OR, Abstract.

2. See Miller, George R., *Pacific Northwest Weather: But My Barometer Says Fair*, 2002, page 26, reference Indian Summer weather.

3. Wind is measured in the direction from which it is blowing. Thus, a southerly wind means the wind is blowing from the south; a northwesterly wind indicates the wind is blowing from the northwest quadrant.

4. In meteorological terms, the situation is referred to as "overrunning" where warmer, moist air is forced aloft over slightly cooler air. This situation occurs quite often along the Pacific Northwest coast.

5. Wind chill is computed using the ambient (actual) temperature of the air and the wind speed. These temperatures are lower than the actual temperature but are an indication of how cold a person "feels."

Chapter**Two**

Along the Pacific Coast

November 15, 1805 to March 23, 1806

The rainy season on the Pacific Northwest Coast normally begins around the latter part of October. Sometimes it's earlier and sometimes it's later. For the Corps of Discovery, it appears to have been about average.

✳ ✳ ✳

"The rainey weather Continued without a longer intermition than 2 hours at a time from the 5th in the morng. untill the 16th is eleven days rain, and the most disagreeable time I have experienced."

William Clark, November 15, 1805,
on north side of Columbia River near Point Ellice
The Journals of the Lewis & Clark Expedition, Volume 6
Gary E. Moulton, Editor

Rain again greeted the Corps of Discovery as dawn came on November 15, 1805, but after a short time a southeasterly wind, blowing down the river sprang up. It also brought with it some sunshine which allowed the party to dry out some of their baggage. The winds subsided, however, and they were able to move around Point Ellice and set up camp, now within full view of the Pacific Ocean. Clark writes, "The after part of this day is fair and calm for the first time since the 5th instant."

At their location (Figure 2.1), the party was experiencing a brief break in the west-northwesterly jet stream as it moved north allowing a weak area of high pressure to settle in over the Pacific Northwest. But several consecutive days without rain on the Pacific Northwest coast in mid-November are rare. Rain returned on November 18, 1805. On November 19, 1805, the main party was camped southeast of Chinook Point. Lewis in his weather table indicates "c.a.r." or "cloudy after rain." Clark's notation for November 19 was, "began to rain a little before day and Continued raining until 11oClock." He comments that he arose that morning, "from under a wet blanket" while camped in what is now Fort

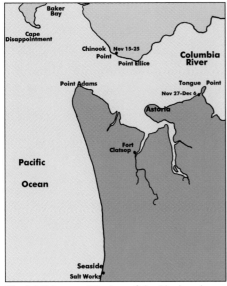

Fig. 2.1 This map of the lower Columbia river shows Astoria, Seaside, Fort Clatsop and where the Corps of Discovery camped in late November and early December.

Canby State Park. Patrick Gass writes for November 19, "We had a cloudy rainy morning." John Ordway, who was with Clark, remarks for November 19, "cloudy a light Sprinkling of rain the later part of last night." Thus, November 19, 1805 was most likely a cloudy day with rain in the morning.

Some discrepancies arise regarding weather for November 20. Clark, who with 10 men, returned from Cape Disappointment to the main camp on the 20th and reported, "Some Rain last night." Lewis in his weather table reported, "rained moderately from 6 A.M." Patrick Gass's entry for the 20th of November, however, was, "We had a fine clear morning. The day continued clear and pleasant throughout." Whitehouse comments, "A clear pleasant morning."[1] And Ordway, "A fair morning."[1] At any rate, the respite was short. Rain and strong south-southeasterly winds returned on November 21 ahead of what appeared to have been a very strong Pacific storm that occurred on November 22, 1805.

✳ ✳ ✳

"...the wind increased to a Storm from the S.S.E. and blew with violence...O! how horriable is the day..."

William Clark, November 22, 1805, southeast of Chinook Point, Pacific County, Washington.
The Journals of the Lewis & Clark Expedition,
Volume 6,
Gary Moulton, Editor.

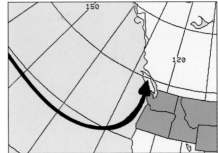

Fig. 2.2 Columbus Day-type storms follow a strong westerly jet stream of around 150 knots as they move across the Pacific Ocean but then curve north along the coasts of Oregon and Washington.

This was most likely one of the strongest storms the party experienced during their stay at the mouth of the Columbia River, and it may have been similar in its track to the infamous Columbus Day Storm of October 12, 1962 along the Pacific Northwest Coast.

These storms move rapidly across the Pacific Ocean under a strong westerly jet stream of 130 to 170 miles per hour toward the Northern California coast. At that point they curve abruptly to the left and move northward along the coasts of Oregon and Washington. (Figure 2.2) Ahead of these storms there is very little east to southeasterly flow except where there are gaps in the Coast Range Mountains. The mouth of the Columbia River, especially where the Corps of Discovery was camped on November 22, is just such a location.

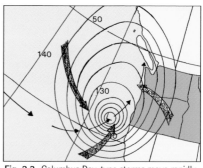

Fig. 2.3 Columbus Day-type storms move rapidly across the Pacific Ocean near latitude 40°N, intensifying, and then curve north along the coasts of Oregon and Washington. Solid lines are isobars.

Lewis's weather entry for November 22 states, "rained all day wind violent from the SE." Clark's notation to this is, "The wind violent from the S.S.E. throwing the water from the R over our camp and rain continued all day." Patrick Gass's entry on November 22 notes a slightly more southerly direction to the wind with, "the wind blew very hard from the south, and the river was rougher than it has ben since we came here. The rain and wind continued all day violent." Whitehouse continues the observations of the 22nd with a slightly different direction to the wind, "A hard Storm arose in the course of last night accompanied with Rain, & it continued raining very hard & the Wind high from the So West." Ordway seems to be in agreement with Whitehouse with his entry on November 22 of, "a hard Storm arose the later part of last night and continues raining and the wind high from the S.W." So, we have some varying directions to the wind on November 22. Who is correct? Most likely all of them.

Our assumption here is that the observations by members of the party occurred at different times on that day.

If the storm on November 22, 1805 was similar to the Columbus Day Storm of October 12, 1962, it would be similar to the following type of scenario. As intense low-pressure areas off the coasts of Oregon and Washington move northward, they are preceded by an area of rapidly falling surface pressure. Strong southeasterly winds are occurring at this time, especially at those locations where there are gaps in the Coast Range

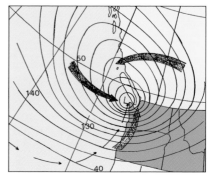

Fig. 2.4 As Columbus Day-type storms move north along the coast, rapidly falling surface pressure ahead of the storm and rapidly rising pressure in the southern quadrant of the storm create strong southeast to southwest winds. Solid lines are isobars.

Mountains, as previously stated. Left in the storm's wake, so to speak, in the southern quadrant of the storm, the winds blow intensely from the south due to the strong pressure gradient from south to north[2] as shown in Figure 2.3.

As the storm center moves north of a location, say the camp of November 22, 1805, the southeasterly wind switches to a more southerly or even south-southwesterly component and even to a southwesterly direction as the wind decreases. Too bad that Lewis and Clark did not have a barometer to measure the air pressure. It is at this point where the winds become strong southerly, that the pressure at a location begins to rapidly increase due to the storm's northward movement past the station and the tight pressure gradient. (Figure 2.4)

These types of storms favor the fall and early winter months. This is when the contrast of temperatures across northern middle latitudes is the strongest. Warm air remains at relatively low middle latitudes, but cold air has already settled in at higher latitudes. This contrast can breed intense low-pressure areas. Another clue might be the storm that occurred on November 21. Columbus Day-type storms are often preceded 18 to 24 hours by a storm of lessor intensity. Remarks on this date by the party seem to indicate this. Lewis's weather entry for this date includes, "rained all last night untill 1 P.M. and Cleared away and was Cloudy without rain." Could the party have been between storms? Clark adds on November 21, "The wind blew hard from the S.E."

A supply of moisture is often available from dying western Pacific typhoons that happen to have moved far enough north to have entered the westerly jet stream. Such was the case on October 12, 1962 as the remains of Typhoon Freda added to the intensity of that storm as it crossed the Pacific Ocean toward the Pacific Northwest. This available moisture contributes to the heavy rain that often occurs with these storms and several of the party remarked on the "moderate" to "hard" rain.

The atmosphere at times seems to overexert itself. A very stormy period is often followed by a stretch of relatively calm, uneventful weather. For the Corps of Discovery it changed from "disagreeable" to, as Patrick Gass mentions on November 24, "The morning was pleasant." Indeed, the first white frost of the fall season had greeted them on the previous morning. They were experiencing another break in the jet stream and the

	Average Temperatures		
	Dec	**Jan**	**Feb**
Astoria			
Maximum	48.4	48.1	50.8
Minimum	36.7	36.7	37.6
Portland			
Maximum	45.4	45.6	50.3
Minimum	35.0	34.2	35.9
The Dalles			
Maximum	41.7	40.8	47.2
Minimum	30.6	29.0	31.8

Fig. 2.5 The average maximum and minimum temperatures for Astoria, Portland and The Dalles reveal significant variations during December, January, and February.

enjoyment of a weak area of high pressure that had moved over the Pacific Northwest with mostly clear skies and some welcome sunshine. They decided to take advantage of the break in the weather and move from their location southeast of Chinook Point.

✳ ✳ ✳

"added to the above advantages in being near the Sea coast one most Strikeing one occurs to me i'e, the Climate which must be from every appearance <must be> much milder than that above the 1st range of Mountains."

William Clark, November 24, 1805,
camped on the north shore of the Columbia River.
The Journals of the Lewis & Clark Expedition, Volume 6,
Gary E. Moulton, Editor

Clark was very much correct. Assuming his first range of mountains was the Coast Range, there is a difference in winter temperatures between Astoria and Portland, Oregon of two to three degrees. In December, the average minimum temperature for Portland is 35.0° while at Astoria it is 36.7°. January's average minimum temperature at Portland is 34.2° compared to 36.7° at Astoria. Average maximum temperatures for December and January at Portland are 45.4° and 45.6°, respectively. This compares to Astoria's 48.4° and 48.1° for the same two months.[3] A difference of two to three degrees might not seem like much, but the moderating effect of the Pacific Ocean is apparent.

If Clark is referring to the Cascade Mountains, the difference is astounding. The Dalles, which was briefly considered as the winter campsite, has an average December maximum temperature of 41.7° and an average monthly minimum of 30.6°. In January the average maximum is 40.8° while the minimum average lowers to 29.0°. Here, the difference between The Dalles and Astoria is 5 to 6 degrees. The Corps of Discovery was wise to stick to the area next to the mild Pacific Ocean. (See Figure 2.5, a table of December, January and February temperatures for Astoria, Portland and The Dalles.) They began to look for a winter campsite near the coast.

Hugging the north shore of the Columbia River on November 25, 1805, the party moved from their camp near Point Chinook around Point Ellice and camped near where they had camped on November 7. The day proved cloudy with spits of rain, but the problem was the strong east-southeast wind blowing down the Columbia River.

An easterly wind at the mouth of the Columbia suggests that the weak area of high pressure that brought them some rainless days had moved east. Once again low pressure offshore with a moist southwesterly jet stream high overhead seems to be the case. The party crossed the river to the south side on November 26.

It had started to rain again the previous evening and now it was raining continuously, but the party did not have to contend with the strong wind and high waves they had encountered on the north side of the river. Here on the south shore of the Columbia River, paddling amongst several islands, the easterly wind was not as strong and the waves could not build to great heights. But weather conditions were slowly changing and as they exited the safety of the islands, the wind increased as well as the rain. They were about to endure another strong Pacific low-pressure system.

✳ ✳ ✳

"Wind Shifted about to the S.W. and blew hard accompanied with hard rain. rained all the last night. About 12 oClock the wind Shifted around to the N.W and blew with great violence the remainder of the day at maney times it blew for 15 or 20 minutes with Such violence that I expected to See trees taken up by the roots, maney were blown down. O! how disagreeable is our Situation dureing this dreadfull weather."

William Clark, November 28, 1805,
on the west side of what is now Tongue Point.
The Journals of the Lewis & Clark Expedition, Volume 6
Gary E. Moulton, Editor

Strong southerly winds precede Pacific storms. Depending on where the center of the low pressure moves inland, these storms can be accompanied by even stronger northwesterly winds. Such was the case on January 9, 1880 when an intense low-pressure center entered the Pacific Northwest almost at the mouth of the Columbia River. Its track was almost due east. Very strong northwesterly winds were recorded as the center of the low pressure passed Astoria and advanced eastward.[4] (See Figure 2.6a and 2.6b for a possible movement of the November 28, 1805 storm.) The party could not have picked a worse place to camp on this particular day, and most of the party remained there until December 7.

The upper-level trough of low

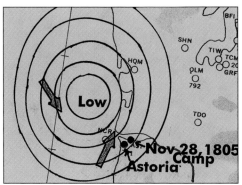

Fig. 2.6a An intense low-pressure system just off the southwest Washington coast would cause strong southwesterly winds at the Corps of Discovery's November 28, 1805 campsite. Solid lines are isobars.

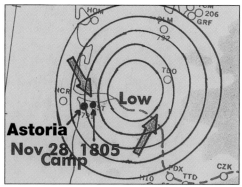

Fig. 2.6b As the low-pressure system moves eastward along the Columbia River, strong southwesterly winds would shift abruptly and blow "with great violence" from a northwesterly direction at the Corps of Discovery's November 28, 1805 campsite. Solid lines are isobars.

pressure must have moved very slowly east for it continued raining hard on November 29, with rain, hail, thunder and lightning during the night. Then on November 30, after some morning showers, the party was greeted with intervals of sunshine between light showers as another area of weak surface high pressure settled over their location. The wind had lulled, allowing Captain Lewis and five men to proceed down the river looking for a suitable winter campsite.

December offered little change in the weather. East-southeasterly winds blowing down the Columbia River occasionally shifted to southwesterly as weak storm fronts passed through the area. Brief heavy rain occurred at times with brief intervals of moderate winds ahead of and with the passage of each storm, but it's unlikely that rain occurred continuously during this period. These storms are usually not strong enough to cause a shift in the surface wind to northwest, but their frequency also offers little in the way of clearing.

Patrick Gass's entry for December 5 was, "Again we had a wet stormy day. There is more wet weather on this coast than I ever knew in any other place; during a month we have had but 3 fair days; and there is no prospect of a change."[5] And indeed there wasn't.

Whitehouse enters in his journal on December 5, "We had hard rain & stormy weather; which was very disagreeable. It continued raining the whole of this day." A stronger storm was approaching the coast. On December 6, Clark writes, "The wind blew hard all last night with a moderate rain, the waves very high, the wind increased & from the S.W.and the rain Continued all day, about Dark the wind Shifted to the North cleared away and became fair weather."

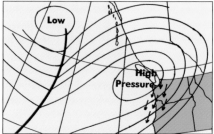

Fig. 2.7 Fair weather greets the Corps of Discovery on the morning of December 7, 1805 as a weak area of high pressure moves onshore ahead of the next Pacific storm front. Solid lines are isobars.

December 7 dawned fair and, relatively speaking, cold. However, a stout wind had sprung up from the northeast as surface high pressure most likely

Fig. 2.8 A replica of the site where the Corps of Discovery camped from December 7, 1805 to March 22, 1806 is located at the Fort Clatsop Memorial south of present Astoria, Oregon.

was pushing into Washington and southern British Columbia. (Figure 2.7) The wind caused some waves on the river, but the party successfully rounded the point (where the town of Astoria currently is located), proceeded around Young's Bay, and up the Lewis and Clark River to where they would build their winter quarters and remain until March 23, 1806.

The site of Fort Clatsop (Figure 2.8) is somewhat protected from strong winds that blow from a west and southwesterly direction. Up until now, the party had been mostly exposed to the wind, and direction was easy to determine. Protected as it is, the winds at Fort Clatsop can blow from almost any direction, but the site is exposed to northeast winds. On December 8, Lewis enters in his log, "wind northeast, cloudy after rain." Clark sets out for the ocean in search of a location where sea water can be boiled for salt. As he nears the ocean on December 9, he encounters, "...a Violent wind from the S.W. untill 10 oClock P.M." They camped that night near what is now Seaside, Oregon.

※ ※ ※

"...verry early I rose and walked on the Shore of the Sea coast and picked up Several Curious Shells. after amuseing my Self for about an hour on the edge of the rageing Seas I returned to the houses"

William Clark, December 10, 1805,
on the beach north of what is now Seaside, Oregon.
The Journals of the Lewis & Clark Expedition, Volume 6,
Gary E. Moulton, Editor.

After a strong Pacific storm, what better form of entertainment is there than walking on the beach, beachcombing. Clark did not refer to it as such, but we can imagine him, like many of us have done, slowly strolling along just looking. The rain did not seem to bother him, and I doubt if it bothers any other serious beachcomber. (Figure 2.9) And rain it did at intervals each day for the rest of December, sometimes moderate to heavy, sometimes light, and at times interspersed with brief sunny periods. Quite likely, the strong west to southwesterly jet stream was reluctant to move.

✳ ✳ ✳

"In the course of the day a good deal of rain fell;
the weather here still continues warm and there has been
no freezing except a little white frost."

Patrick Gass, December 14, 1805,
camped at Fort Clatsop.
The Journals of the Lewis & Clark Expedition, Volume 10,
Gary E. Moulton, Editor.

Winter weather along the coasts of Washington and Oregon is indeed mild due to a prevailing westerly wind. For cold, freezing weather to occur along the Pacific Northwest Coast, there must be an interruption of the onshore westerly flow. Occasionally, upper-level troughs of low pressure bring with them air that is cold enough to lower the freezing level close to the surface. They often stall along the Pacific Northwest coast. This appears to

Fig. 2.9 Sometimes it's only a lone gull that greets the early beachcomber, such as William Clark on December 10, 1805, near what is now Seaside, Oregon.

have been the case during mid December. It began, however, with a strange and speculative occurrence on December 16.

✳ ✳ ✳

"The rain Contines, with Tremendious gusts of wind, which is Tremds. The winds violent Trees falling in every derection, whorl winds, withs gusts of rain Hail & Thunder. A tempestuous disagreeable day."

William Clark, December 16, 1805,
near Fort Clatsop.
The Journals of the Lewis & Clark Expedition, Volume 6
Gary E. Moulton, Editor.

Thunder and hail are indicative of an unstable atmosphere. An unstable atmosphere is one of the key ingredients required to produce tornadoes. Could the Corps of Discovery be the first Americans to have witnessed an Oregon tornado?

TABLE 2.1 FUJITA TORNADO SCALE (Estimated miles per hour)	
F0 40-72	light damage
F1 73-112	moderate damage
F2 113-157	considerable damage
F3 158-206	severe damage
F4 207-260	devastation
F5 greater than 260	incredible damage

Certainly, there is not enough data to support this speculation. But the expression, "trees falling in every derection, whorl winds," raises the question.

Tornadoes do occur along the coastal sections of Oregon and Washington. Several over the last 50 years have occurred at Long Beach in southwest Washington, and at Astoria and Seaside, Oregon. On January 5, 1998 an F0 tornado touched down in Seaside, Oregon. An F0 tornado on September 15, 1996, near Seaside injured one person. Another F0 tornado occurred on September 12, 1997 north of Long Beach near Oysterville in Pacific County, Washington. (See Table 2.1 for an explanation of tornado severity.) Indeed, even a minor tornado is a rare event along the coast, but could the Corps of Discovery have been the first to have observed one? We will never know, but it is fun to speculate.

But the event that caught the attention of the Lewis and Clark Expedition was the switch to a slightly colder weather regime. Snow fell on the party for the first time the evening of December 17. Clark writes on December 18, "rained and Snowed alturnitely all the last night and the gusts of Snow and hail continue untill 12oClock, Cold and a dreadfull day wind hard and unsettled." The entry by Gass on December 18 was, "Snow fell last night about an inch deep."

The cold upper-level low that plagued the party, Figure 2.10, was reluctant to move east. Entries for the next few days indicate showers, hail, rain and snow mixed. The low snow level was bringing snow to the Coast Range Mountains. Clark indicates this with his comment on December 17, "The mountain which lies S.E of this is covered with Snow to day." The cold low obviously moved east on December 21, but was replaced by the jet stream from the west-southwest with continuous rain. Clark wrote on December 21,

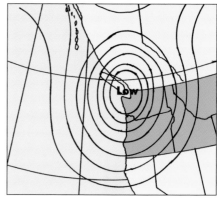

Fig. 2.10 A cold upper-level area of low pressure moving slowly east was the likely cause of the inclement weather the Corps of Discovery experienced December 16-20, 1805.

"rain as usial last night and all day to day moderately." The weather begins to warm after the brief cool period. "We discover that part of our last Supply of meat is Spoiling from the wompg [warmth] of the weather...," Clark enters on December 22. There was not much movement north or south to the jet stream that was blowing from a west-southwest and west-northwest direction. It would soon cool off as another cold trough of low pressure aloft approached the area.

✳ ✳ ✳

"rained all last night and moderately to day with Several Showers of Hail accompanied with hard Claps of Thunder and Sharp Lightning.

Meriwether Lewis, December 23, 1805,
at Fort Clatsop.
The Journals of the Lewis & Clark Expedition, Volume 6,
Gary E. Moulton, Editor

Thunderstorms are not as common an occurrence in the Pacific Northwest as they are in the Rocky Mountain states and all of the middle and eastern areas of the United States. An increase in number occurs in spring and summer east of the Cascade Mountains, while west of the Cascade Mountains the winter season seems to be the most active. Winter thunderstorms along the Pacific Northwest coast are short. (Figure 2.11, shows a thunderstorm near the mouth of Columbia River.) Often it is only one or two claps of thunder that are heard and the storm moves quickly east, or dissipates. Astoria, Oregon averages about three thunderstorms total for the three-month period of November through January. The Corps of Discovery, however, records two thunderstorms in each

Fig. 2.11 A strong thunderstorm nears the mouth of the Columbia River as seen from the Long Beach Peninsula.

of these months. Is this a significant increase over today's averages? Probably not, but a reason for the difference should be noted.

The Corps of Discovery was often exposed to the elements with no other distracting sounds. Twentieth century weather observers were inside a building and exposed to a variety of sounds both inside and out that would often prevent them from hearing a clap of thunder. Also, the weather regime plays an important part in thunderstorm development. When the precipitation total is below average, the thunderstorm frequency will likely be below average, with none reported during some winters.

※ ※ ※

"The day proved Showerey wet and disagreeable."

William Clark, December 25, 1805,
at Fort Clatsop.
The Journals of the Lewis & Clark Expedition, Volume 6,
Gary E. Moulton, Editor.

There would be no white Christmas for the Corps of Discovery. And the occurrence of a white Christmas west of the Cascade Mountains today is very rare, especially along the coast. No, the day was just like most Christmas Days are today—rainy and wet. The only item of weather that one might consider remarkable was one of the two recorded thunderstorms with lightning that occurred Christmas night. Lewis's weather entry for December 26 was, "wind southwest; rain after thunder and lightning." Rain continued off and on at Fort Clatsop through the end of 1805.

✳ ✳ ✳

"the changes of the weather are exceedingly suddon. sometimes tho'
seldom the sun is visible for a few moments the next it hails & rains,
then ceases, and remains cloudy the wind blows and it again rains;
the wind blows by squalls most generally and is almost invariable
from the S.W. these visicitudes of the weather happen two three
or more times half a day.

Meriwether Lewis, January 1, 1806,
camped at Fort Clatsop.
The Journals of the Lewis & Clark Expedition, Volume 6,
Gary E. Moulton, Editor.

All Oregonians are familiar with the cliché: "If you don't like the weather now, just wait a few minutes or move." It appears that Lewis also could have used the cliché. After a winter storm has passed, Pacific Northwest weather is often unsettled with frequent showers, squalls, interspersed with brief sunny periods. At this point, precipitation increases the farther one moves inland from the coast and the higher in elevation. The reason for this is the cool, moist air from the ocean is forced aloft as it begins to cross the Coast Range Mountains. Clouds form and precipitation soon follows. A typical weather regime is seen in Figure 2.12.

Fig. 2.12 As clouds are forced over the Coast Range Mountains, the air cools, clouds form and precipitation increases from values recorded at coastal locations.

"The Sun rose fair this morning for the first time for Six weeks past."

William Clark, January 3, 1806.

"Since our arrival in this neighbourhood on the 7th of November,
we have experienced one slight white frost only which happened
on the morning of the 16th of that month."

Meriwether Lewis, January 3, 1806.
The Journals of the Lewis & Clark Expedition, Volume 6,
Gary E. Moulton, Editor

For the most part, the two Captains agree on their weather entries. But on January 13, 1806, when referring to prevailing winds on Baker Bay, they mildly disagree. Lewis writes, "The bay in which this trade is carryed on is spacious and commodious, and perfectly secure from all except the S. and S.E. winds, these however are the most prevalent and strong winds in the Winter season." Clark, however, enters in his log, "The Bay in which the trade is Carried on is Spacious and Commodious and perfectly Secure from all except the S.& S.E. Winds and those blow but Seldom. The most prevalent & Strong winds are from the S W & N W in the Winter Season." So, who is correct? Let's give both captains some credit.

At the Astoria airport the prevailing wind during November, December and January is east to southeast. This is indeed not a favorable direction for anchoring ships in Baker Bay. The long fetch down the Columbia River would provide large waves and rough conditions, especially during tidal changes. The strongest winds, however, with their associated gusts are from the south to southwest. The bay is somewhat protected from west to northwest winds. It appears that Clark's entry is likely tainted by his memory of the storm of November 28 while camped on the south side of the Columbia River. This storm blew with violence and uprooted trees. The wind was blowing from the northwest.

How quickly we forget. When references are made to the weather, it's often the extremes that we remember. It might be a particularly hot day; one with copious rain and perhaps thunder; a large snowfall. We remember that one camping trip where it rained continuously, and forget about the many where the weather was beautiful. We forget about all those days when the weather was "normal" or bland. We remember those terrible storms. It's the same with weather forecasts. The correct ones are never remembered; those inaccurate reports are the ones people usually remember.

Lewis and Clark had no forecasts, but they did have their observations and those of other members of their party. From the above quotations, they appear to have been caught in this world of remembering only what stuck in their minds. And who can blame them? They were not native residents of the Pacific Northwest. They came from a land

Fig. 2.13 During the winter months, gray, damp skies are a familiar site at the mouth of the Columbia River.

where continuous clouds and rain for five days straight is a rare occurrence. They were wet, cold and hungry. Their clothes were rotting. They had arrived at a location where precipitation is the rule from November to May, not the exception. It seems likely they would complain about the rain and forget the few sunny days. Today, the majority of those residents west of the Cascade Mountains are in this category. And who can blame them if they look out at a gray, damp and dreary Pacific Ocean like that shown in Figure 2.13.

It did rain on the Corps of Discovery, but not all the time. Patrick Gass writes on November 24, 1805, "The morning was fine with some white frost. As this was a fine clear day..." and on December 8, 1805, "We had a fine fair morning with some white frost." On November 25, Whitehouse records, "We had a clear pleasant morning," and on December 7, "This morning clear and cold." Ordway on November 20, "a fair morning," and on December 29, "a fair day." It may have rained a lot with some rain recorded on many of the days, but not for 40 days and 40 nights!

From January 6 to 10, 1806, the party enjoyed several rainless days. Clark had left Fort Clatsop and journeyed to the coast south of Tillamook Head to view a whale that had beached. Throughout this time, both men record a northeast to southeast wind. Was the jet stream changing its location and orientation? Was this fair, cool period a clue of what was in store, weatherwise, for the party later in January? Maybe, but for the next two weeks, the pattern of rain and wind off and on was the case, interspersed with some fair and cloudy days. And, it appeared to have been mild.

✳ ✳ ✳

"weather perfectly temperate I never experienced a winter
so warm as the present has been."

"weather warm, we could do very well without fire. I am satisfyed that
the murcury would stand at 55 a.0."

Meriwether Lewis, January 13 and 14, 1806,
camped at Fort Clatsop.
The Journals of the Lewis & Clark Expedition, Volume 6,
Gary E. Moulton, Editor.

"when the sun is said to shine ore the weather fair it is to be understood that it bearly casts a shaddow, and that the atmosphere is haizy of a milkey white colour."

Meriwether Lewis, January 23, 1806.

Cirrostratus clouds give the sky a milky-white appearance through which the sun shines, but not very brightly, just enough to cast a light shadow. Lewis was probably observing a sky filled with cirrostratus clouds 5 or 6 miles above the earth.

It was unfortunate that the party's last thermometer was broken somewhere in Idaho by the box striking against a tree. Temperature data would have been a valuable addition to their entries. Nevertheless, we can be assured that Lewis was pretty accurate with his 55 degrees. The temperature of the Pacific Ocean in January off the coast of Oregon is in the 50s. Air near the surface blowing over the water quickly assumes that temperature. Lewis's astute entry for January 12 adds credence to his observational skills when he writes, "the wind from any quarter off the land or along the N.W. Coast causes the air to become much cooler." Having no thermometer, his temperature estimating skills would be of great use later on in January.

Except for a few frosts, the Corps of Discovery experienced little cold weather. A jet stream blowing from a west-southwest and west-northwest direction had plagued them with storm after storm since their arrival at the Pacific Ocean. Only briefly did weak areas of high pressure sneak in to provide them with brief periods of sunny weather. Little did the party know, however, that the jet stream was undergoing major changes—changes that would bring them the coldest weather since their stay at Fort Mandan in North Dakota during the winter of 1804-05.

✳ ✳ ✳

"the ground covered with snow this morning 1/2 inch deep ice on the water in the canoes 1/4 of an inch thick. it is now preceptably coulder than it has been this winter."

Meriwether Lewis, January 25, 1806,
at Fort Clatsop.
The Journals of the Lewis & Clark Expedition, Volume 6,
Gary E. Moulton, Editor

The weather had turned colder. Arctic air from somewhere in the interior of Canada or Alaska had invaded the Pacific Northwest and made its way to the coast. Below-freezing temperatures are a rare event along the coast. It takes a major change in the orientation of the jet stream for this to happen. Instead of a westerly flow of air aloft, the flow changes to a northerly direction at elevations from 2 to 6 miles above the earth. (Figure 2.14) This weather pattern is favorable for bringing cold, arctic surface air southward into the Pacific Northwest. Low-level winds next to the surface change also, from onshore or westerly to a more easterly direction, or offshore. And with cold air from the interior reaching the coast, there is a good possibility of snow.

Lewis enters in his journal for January 26, 1806, "coulder than it has been... the snow this evening is 4 3/4 inches deep, the icesickles of 18 inches in length continued suspended from the eves of the houses during the day. it now appears something like winter for the first time this season." And with cold clear air, the atmosphere is sparkling.

Lewis's entry for January 27 was, "the sun shone more bright this morning

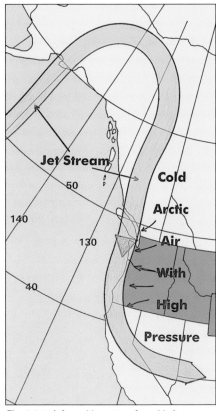

Fig. 2.14 A favorable pattern for cold air to invade the Pacific Northwest is a strong northerly jet stream that brings cold arctic air southward over Oregon and Washington.

than it has done since our arrival at this place." And the snow continued to fall. An additional entry for January 27 stated, "the snow since 4 P.M. yesterday has increased to the depth of 6 inches, and this morning is perceptibly the coldest that we have had. I suspect the Murcury would stand at about 20° above naught." And on January 28, "it is the couldest night that we have had, and I suppose the murcury this morning would have stood as low as 15° above 0." [6]

A thermometer reading in the teens at Astoria is not your normal winter occurrence. Snow, also, could be considered a somewhat rare event. Although Astoria averages about 4 inches each year, it normally records an inch here, an inch there, etc., due to very cold air aloft passing quickly through associated with an upper-level trough of low pressure. This type of snowfall quickly melts. In 1806, however, the snow remained on the ground from January 24 to February 8. It was an unusually long and very cold spell for coastal locations.

Lewis had put out a vessel filled with water on the night of January 27. The next morning he reported, "the vessel was only 2 inches deep and it feized the whole thickness; how much more it might have frozen had the vessel been deeper is therefore out of my power to decide." His temperature estimates seem to have been verified. They were substantiated with his entry for January 31, "Sent a party of eight men up the river this morning to renew their surch for the Elk, and also to hunt; they proceded but a few miles before they found the river So obstructed with ice that they were obliged to return." Rivers do not freeze over very often at coastal locations.

✳ ✳ ✳

"The Winds from the Land brings us could and clear weather
while those obliquely along either coast or off the Oceans
bring us warm damp cloudy and rainy weather. the hardest winds
are always from the S.W."

Meriwether Lewis, January 31, 1806,
at Fort Clatsop.
The Journals of the Lewis & Clark Expedition, Volume 6,
Gary E. Moulton, Editor

Once again one has to be impressed with Captain Lewis's weather observations and meteorological knowledge. On only rare occasions would this not be true. During winter, cold, clear weather at the coast does arrive on winds that blow from an easterly direction. Rain and cloudy weather generally move in from the Pacific Ocean.

Cold arctic outbreaks, as they are called by meteorologists, rarely last more than a week in the Pacific Northwest west of the Cascade Mountains. The Corps of Discovery, however, experienced an exception to that. In fact, the length of the cold spell leads one to believe that there might have been two, or perhaps three, sieges of arctic air that invaded the Pacific Northwest. On January 30, the wind switches briefly around to north and then to west, bringing snow. However, on January 31, it shifts again to northeast and remains from this quadrant until late in the day on February 2.

During the night of February 2 and the early morning hours of February 3, the party probably experienced some freezing rain.[7] Lewis's entry for February is, "the rain which feel in the latter part of the night freized and formed a slight incrustation on the snow which fell some days past and also on the boughs of the trees." Often, this is a signal that the cold spell is weakening. But Lewis's entry for 4 PM on February 3 records a northeast wind.

On that afternoon Drewyer (Drouillard) and La Page (LePage) had returned and reported to have killed seven elk near Adams Point. Lewis writes, "direct Sergt. pryor to go in quest of the meat, the wind was so high that they were unable to set out untill a little before sunset." The cold northeast wind was bringing with it another surge of arctic air. On February 4, Lewis enters, "the last night clear and could the Netul[8] frozen over in several places." And on February 6, "very cold last night think it reather the coldest night that we have had."

The Corps of Discovery was greeted with a blast of arctic air to the coast of northern Oregon that lasted for two weeks. Temperatures were estimated to have lowered into the teens. One can only specu-

Some variations exist as to the actual depth of the snow reported while the party was at Fort Clatsop. Patrick Gass's entry for January 25 reports snow depth of 8 inches and 9 inches on the 27th. Whitehouse says, "5 inches deep on the level," on January 26. Ordway concurs with his observation.

This is quite understandable considering where they are camped. Snow, especially if it is cold, dry snow, which appears the case if Lewis's temperature readings are to be taken into account, will form drifts if there is any wind. As the wind blows around obstacles such as trees, their dwellings, it will accumulate in some areas, and in others be swept almost clean. Also, hunters leaving the camp and venturing inland would have encountered different snow depths, usually greater.

Today, observers who measure snow are asked to measure it in several different places and take an average.

"One of the first spells of unusual weather I had to record came in January 1930. Cold, clear weather set in on January 6 and continued through the rest of the month, with temperatures down below freezing nearly every night.

Ice began forming in the Columbia River and before long had created ice barriers along the north shore, around Altoona and Brookfield, and around Puget Island."

Fred Andrus, Daily Astorian, January 6, 1977

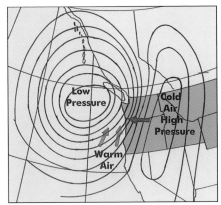

Fig. 2.15 As cold arctic air begins to recede, warm south to southwesterly winds begin to prevail, first along the coast and finally spreading into interior western valleys.

late as to how far the mercury would have lowered farther inland in the Willamette Valley and east of the Cascade Mountains near The Dalles. It would seem possible that near-zero readings would have occurred in the Willamette Valley and far below zero east of the Cascade Mountains.

But on February 7, 1806 the arctic air finally began its retreat. Surface winds switched around to the southwest at Fort Clatsop bringing clouds and warmer temperatures. High over their heads, the jet stream was taking up its normal position from a westerly direction. But inland, the change would have been slower. Had the party set up their winter camp at the west end of the Columbia River Gorge, they likely would have been battling snowdrifts many feet deep as strong, cold easterly winds pouring though this gap in the Cascade Mountains collided with warmer air.[9] If the choice had been near The Dalles, they would have experienced another winter with sub-zero temperatures much like they experienced at Fort Mandan the winter before. What would have been the fate of the Corps of Discovery had they set up their winter camp at either location?

On the Pacific Northwest coast, however, the ocean was performing its moderating act. Mild ocean air was pushing onshore. (Figure 2.15) Lewis enters in his log on February 8, 1806, "the feeling of the air and other appearances seem to indicate, that the rigor of the winter have passed; it is so warm that we are apprehensive that our meat will spoil."

For the next few days, a series of storms passed the site at Fort Clatsop bringing a return to the rain

During the winter of 1861-62, perhaps the most severe ever in Washington and Oregon, miners returning from the gold fields of Idaho with gold in their pockets froze to death in eastern Oregon. During the severe winter of 1884-85, a train was stranded in the Columbia River Gorge at Viento from December 17 to January 5 due to cold and heavy snow.

and wind. Occasionally the storm had enough cold air aloft to lower the snow level to near the surface. The party reported snow on the ground in the morning on February 10, 14, 16 and 17, but it soon melted as is common with most mid-February snowstorms. Hail also was reported on several days indicating an unstable atmosphere that had the sun shining for brief periods of time.

Strong southwesterly winds occurred from February 18-21. These winds produced high waves on the bay leading to the Columbia River. Rain accompanied the winds. Then, after a brief respite on the 22nd and 23rd of February, the party was due for another storm. On the 25th of February, Lewis writes, "the wind violent all night and this morning." February's unsettled weather fathered by a west-southwesterly jet stream continued into March.

"even the Easterly winds which have heretofore given us the only fair weather which we have enjoyed seem now to have lost their influence in this rispect."

This entry by Captain Lewis on March 6 is a keen bit of meteorological knowledge. Easterly winds at the coast can show a slight increase in the winter months, due to slightly higher pressure inland and slightly lower pressure off the coast. During the spring months of March, April and May, the pressure inland begins decreasing and easterly winds are not as frequent. There are exceptions to this as the party will experience in their journey up the Columbia River, but Lewis' observation is quite correct.

* * *

"A high mountain is Situated S60°W. about 18 miles from Fort Clatsop[10] on which there has been Snow Since Nov."

William Clark, March 5, 1806,
at Fort Clatsop.
The Journals of the Lewis & Clark Expedition, Volume 6,
Gary E. Moulton, Editor

The stormy weather, with a relatively low freezing level, was obviously depositing copious amounts of snow in the mountains, quite likely down to elevations of 1,000 to 2,000 feet. Deep winter snowfall in the mountains and foothills of the Pacific Northwest often results in rivers rising out of their banks with flooding caused by the melting of the snow. The Corps of Discovery, however, would not be able to observe this due to their location. The rivers near Fort Clatsop do not have a large enough watershed. The Nehalem River, farther south, would show some fluctuation in height. The party did not get this far south. It would be different on their journey back up the Columbia River.

The warming over the first few days of March may have started the snow melting at locations slightly higher in elevation. Lewis writes on March 1, "a great part of this day was so warm that fire was unnecessary, notwithstanding it's being cloudy and raining." Again on March 3, he enters, "air perfectly temperate." But that would soon change.

Another slow-moving, cold upper-level trough was sending the brief warm period on its way and replacing it with colder, unsettled weather. "The air is considerably colder this morng but nothing like freizing," Lewis writes on March 5. And again on March 6, he enters, "air is perceptably colder than it has been since the 1st inst." The weather was unsettled as cold unstable air once more invaded the Pacific Northwest.

"Sudden changes & frequent, during the day, scarcly any two hours of the same discription," Lewis writes on the 7th of March. The cold, unstable air began producing hail and snow showers that covered the ground white on the 8th and 9th and again on the 11th in the morning. The party is experiencing a typical March in the Pacific Northwest.

On March 11, however, the cold, upper-level trough is moving eastward. The day ends with a slight northeast breeze portending some fair weather. It was frosty in the morning on the 12th and 13th and Lewis enters on March 14, "yesterday and last night were the most perfectly fair wether we have seen at this place."

Even today after a period of inclement, showery, stormy weather those first few days when the sun does shine uninterrupted for a day or two, Pacific Northwest residents are filled with energy. Garden plans are made, golf clubs dusted off, and the hint of summer activities sends our minds wandering. Was the party getting a touch of "spring fever" just like we do? Their thoughts, however, are likely those of leaving their location for over three months and returning home.

But alas, our hopes, and certainly theirs, are quickly scuttled. March 17 brought another round of showers, hail and snow. "frequent and sudden changes," Lewis writes. This period of stormy weather continued for several days. Each day produced more rain and hail and southwest wind. It was preventing them from getting their canoes and supplies ready for the trip up river. It also may have prevented their coming in contact with a Russian ship, *Juno*, out of New Archangel (Sitka) that tried for several days to cross the treacherous Columbia River Bar.[11] Lewis enters in his journal on March 20, "It continued to rain and blow so violently today that nothing could be done towards forwarding our departure."

The strong storm abated on the 21st of March. It continued showery, however, even into the morning of the 23rd, the day the party left their "home-away-from-home" and started back up the Columbia River. What vicissitudes of the weather would they encounter on this the first leg of their journey back across the Rocky Mountains?

1. Lewis's weather table for November 20 has "f.a.r." or "fair after rain." He has no weather **remark** entered for November 19, 1805. Quite likely, his remark for November 20 ("rained moderately after 6 A. M.") should be November 19. This would fit better with Clark and other members of the party's entries for those two days. November 20, 1805 appears to have been a pleasant day after rain the night before. Rain began again that night, however.

2. The weather reporting station at the airport in Astoria, Oregon recorded a peak gust of 96 mph during the Columbus Day Storm of October 12, 1962. Newport, on the central Oregon coast registered 138 mph. Naselle, Washington reported 160 mph.

3. Monthly temperature averages are based on climatic normals for 1971-2000.

4. The January 9, 1880 storm was very intense. The lowest pressure ever recorded in Oregon (28.45 inches) occurred during this storm at Astoria.

5. Patrick Gass probably would have made a good weather observer. On the average Astoria, Oregon records between 5 to 6 clear days during November and December, about 9 partly cloudy days and the rest, 46 to 47, cloudy. On the average 43 of the 61 days in November and December 0.01 inch of precipitation falls.

6. Since 1953 when observations began at the airport, the coldest reading at Astoria has been 6°F.

7. Freezing rain is rain that freezes when it strikes objects that are below freezing. The precipitation may begin as snow higher up in the atmosphere, fall through a layer of warm air that is above freezing and melt. Then as it falls through a very shallow layer of air next to the surface that is below freezing, it freezes on impact since the objects it strikes are below freezing.

8. The Netul River is the Lewis and Clark River on which they were camped.

9. On January 9, 1980, 39 inches of snow fell at Bonneville Dam in a 24-hour period.

10. As Moulton states on page 384, this description would place the mountain in the Pacific Ocean. Clark obviously means "East" rather than "West." The mountain thus becomes Saddle Mountain as mentioned in Chapter 1.

11. See Moulton, Volume 6, page 432.

Chapter**Three**

From the Pacific Coast
to the Rocky Mountains

March 23, 1806 to July 1, 1806

On March 23, 1806, The Corps of Discovery left Fort Clatsop. I have been to the coast many times and often it seems that just as I am getting ready to leave, the skies clear, the sun comes out and the weather is beautiful. I'm wondering if the members of the expedition thought the same. Indeed, they were delayed in leaving their camp by the rain and wind that morning. They just made it around the point where present-day Astoria is located and around Tongue Point. Lewis writes in his journal on that day, "it became fair at 12 OCk. and continued cloudy and fair by intervals without rain till night." It appeared the weather may have given the party a sunny farewell.

※ ※ ※

"not withstanding the repeeted fall of rain which has fallen almost Constantly Since we passed the long narrows on the [blank] of Novr. Last[1] indeed w[e] have had only [blank] days fair weather since that time."

William Clark, March 23, 1806,
leaving Fort Clatsop.
The Journals of the Lewis & Clark Expedition, Volume 7,
Gary E. Moulton, Editor

The common theme that surrounds the Lewis and Clark Expedition was that they spent a horrible (disagreeable) winter at the mouth of the Columbia River, surviving rainstorm after rainstorm, soaking wet with clothes rotting. But was their November through March any wetter than the same period today? If we substitute just a few of the "fair" entries with "sunny," it might not be as bad as they portrayed, or was it?

The period from November 1 through March 31 contains 151 days, 152 during leap years.[2] Lewis in his weather table, mentions rain on 24 days in

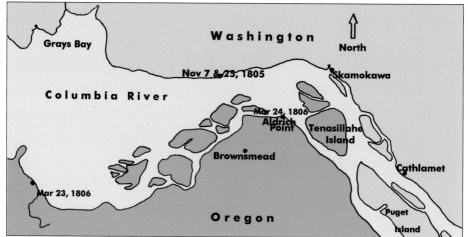

Fig. 3.1 The above map of the lower Columbia River shows the campsites of November 7 & 25, 1805 and March 23 & 24, 1806.

November, all 31 days in December, 22 days in January,[3] 21 days in February[4] and 26 days in March for total "rain days" of 124. Throw in the four days with snow being recorded and the result is 128 days out of a possible 151 where some form of precipitation was recorded.[5]

If we use the period November 2003 through March 2004 as a recent comparison, the National Weather Service Station at Astoria recorded 116 days during that period when at least 0.01 of an inch of precipitation was measured. Also during that same period, there were 11 days when only a trace[6] of precipitation was measured, or one might say 127 "rain days." At Astoria on the average, 0.01 inch precipitation occurs on 21 days in November, 22 days in December, 22 days in January, 19 days in February and 21 days in March for a total of 105 days.

The average precipitation at Astoria in inches for each of the five months is: November 10.49, December 10.79, January 10.28, February 7.67 and March 7.33 or 46.56 inches.[7] The total for November 2003 was 9.75; for December 2003, 9.87; January 2004, 12.90; February 2004, 6.97 and March 2004, 5.47 for a total of 44.96 inches or roughly one and one-half inches below the long-term average for Astoria. Thus, the period November 2003 through March 2004 could be considered near normal for that period.

During November 1996 through March 1997, 63.89 inches of precipitation was recorded at Astoria. During that period, November recorded 24 days with at least 0.01 precipitation, December 27, January 23, February 17 and March 27 for a total of 118 days with measurable precipitation. Add to that three days with only a trace and we have 121 "rain days" or close to the "rain days" that the Lewis and Clark Expedition experienced. I am sure coastal residents during that winter were remarking, "Oh! How horrible and disagreeable is the weather!"

During November 1955 through March 1956, over 70 inches of rain was recorded at Astoria. November's total was 14.64 inches, December's 16.57, January's 17.09, February's 9.32 and March's 13.47. During that period, measurable precipitation was recorded on 119 days and a "trace" of rain was indicated on 10 days. That makes a total of 129 "rain days." The Corps of Discovery's record is broken by one day. This could certainly fall into that "disagreeable" category. And also during the winter of 2003/2004.

From all indications, however, it does appear that the party experienced a wet winter camped near and on the shores of the Pacific Ocean with rainfall above the current average. But it may not have been a record. Precipitation records at Astoria go back to 1853 with several years in between missing. Until 1953, observations were taken downtown at several locations. Since then, official weather observations have been taken at the Astoria airport. The author doubts whether there would be much variation in total amounts between the two locations. During several of those years since 1853 the five-month total exceeded 70 inches and exceeded 60 inches many times. There have also been some "dry" periods. By all indications, an El Niño event governed the weather a year prior to the Corps of Discovery's visit. El Niño winters are generally dry winters in the Pacific Northwest. If the winter of 1804-1805 was dry, I wonder if the natives had told them, "You should have been here last year!"

With Fort Clatsop and the Pacific Ocean behind them, the party may have thought they were leaving the wet, rainy weather. Not quite so. The party camped for the night just east of Tongue Point. Rain began during the

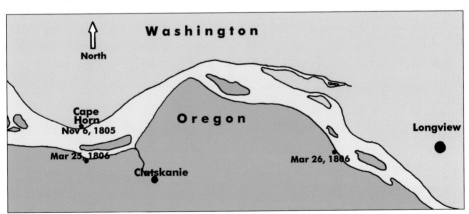

Fig. 3.2 The above map shows a portion of the lower Columbia River west of Longview, Washington and the campsites of November 6, 1805 and March 25 and 26, 1806.

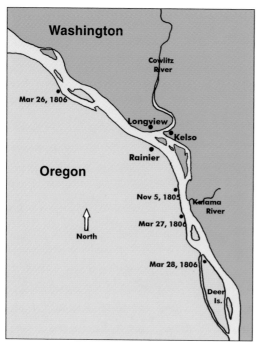

Washington

Cowlitz River

Mar 26, 1806

Longview

Kelso

Rainier

Oregon

Nov 5, 1805

Kalama River

↑ North

Mar 27, 1806

Mar 28, 1806

Deer Is.

Fig. 3.2a This map shows the Columbia River near the Kelso/Longview area and campsites of November 5, 1805 and March 26-28, 1806.

night and continued during the morning of March 24 as a weak Pacific storm front moved through the area, The weather, however, cleared up and the party was greeted with some sunshine and westerly winds paddling along the south shore of the Columbia River through several islands toward their camp on March 24 near Aldrich Point (Figure 3.1). It was a "disagreeably cold" morning on March 25, 1806, Lewis entered in his journal as the party prepared to leave their camp near Aldrich Point. For most of March 25, 1806 they battled a strong easterly wind blowing down the river. The going was tough against a strong wind and to add to the party's woes, by afternoon it had begun to rain. They were not able to paddle fast enough to escape another rapidly advancing Pacific storm.

The river itself was beginning to rise from spring snowmelt and the current was strong. Patrick Gass writes on March 25, "At this time (in the afternoon) the wind rose and blew very hard accompanied with rain." It must have been a miserable trip to their camp of March 25 just west of Clatskanie, Oregon, across from Cape Horn. (Figure 3.2)

✳ ✳ ✳

"The wind blew so hard this morning that we delayed untill 8 A.M."

Meriwether Lewis, March 26, 1806,
leaving their camp west of Clatskanie, Oregon.
The Journals of the Lewis & Clark Expedition, Volume 7
Gary E. Moulton, Editor

The wind, however, had now switched around to a more favorable direction from the northwest, indicating the passage of yet another Pacific storm front. They were granted a short respite from the rain and greeted with a little sunshine, but by afternoon the wind had switched around to the southeast.

Could yet another siege of stormy weather be approaching? Quite likely, since it rained for most of the next few days.

✳ ✳ ✳

"the morning was very cold wind Sharp and keen off the rainge of Mountains to the East Covered with snow. the river is now riseing very fast and retards our progress very much as we are compelled to keep out at Some distance in the Current to clear the bushes, and fallin trees and drift logs makeing out from the Shore."

William Clark, March 29, 1805,
on the Columbia River somewhere near present-day Woodland, Washington.
The Journals of the Lewis & Clark Expedition, Volume 7
Gary E. Moulton, Editor.

The Columbia River was rising. The melting of winter snow in the mountains, and certainly the foothills and lower elevations, had begun. Clark also enters on this day, "we prosued their advice and Crossed into the mouth of the Chah-wah-na-hi-ooks River[8] which is about 200 yards wide and a great portion of water into the columbia at this time it being high." (Figure 3.3) Whitehouse on March 30 enters in his log, "the River still continuing rising, and is so high, that the tide has no Effect. We saw considerable quantity of drift wood floating down the River." Gass adds to this with, "The river is very high, over-flowing all its banks."

The Columbia River drains an area of 219,000 square miles in the states of Washington, Oregon,

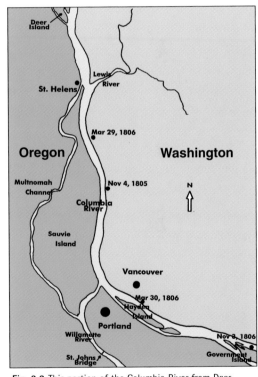

Fig. 3.3 This portion of the Columbia River from Deer Island to Government Island shows campsites of November 3 & 4, 1805 and March 29 & 30, 1806.

Idaho, Montana, Wyoming, Nevada, and Utah. An additional 39,500-square-mile portion of the basin, or about 15%, is within Canada. Depending on climatic conditions, the spring mountain snowmelt begins in March at lower elevations and normally reaches a peak in late May or early June. The Lewis and Clark party was experiencing an early rise on the river that was likely related to melting of a low-elevation snowpack that had accumulated over the winter.

The weather cleared enough for the party to view the various mountain peaks on the 30th. Lewis enters on that date, "we had a view of mount St. helines and Mount Hood. the 1st is the most noble looking object of it's kind in nature. it's figure is a regular cone. both these mountains are perfectly covered with snow." He adds in his weather remarks, "weather moderately warm."

After camping across from either Hayden or Tomahawk Island in present-day Vancouver, Washington on March 30, 1806, the party proceeded a short distance above the Washougal River on March 31 to their camp of the next five days. (Figure 3.4) The weather continued fair.

✳ ✳ ✳

"From the best opinion I could form of the State of the Columbia on the 1st of April it was about 9 feet higher than when we decended it in the beginning of November last."

Meriwether Lewis, April 1, 1806,
while camped near Washougal, Washington.
The Journals of the Lewis & Clark Expedition, Volume 7,
Gary E. Moulton, Editor

Once again, Lewis's keen observation is apparent. The flow on the Columbia River in 1806 was unregulated. Today, the flow is highly regulated by several dams on it and its major tributaries. Thus it becomes difficult to compare events then and now. But some observations can certainly be noted.

The average flow at The Dalles in April is around 200,000 cubic feet per second (CFS). In November the average flow is 100,000 CFS. Using this

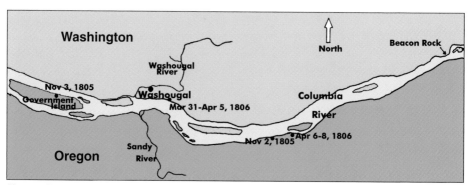

Fig. 3.4 The map shows campsites along the Columbia River for November 2 & 3, 1805 and March 31 to April 8, 1806 from Government Island to Beacon Rock.

comparison downstream at Vancouver, Washington that difference translates into around a three-foot difference.[9] Was Lewis's observation too large? No.

Quite likely a dry summer had prevailed over the Pacific Northwest in 1805. Indeed, precipitation in September and October appeared to be sparse except for a couple of storms. Some of the lowest levels that occur on the Columbia River at its downstream locations come during October after a dry, or below normal precipitation, summer and early fall. Then, should an early melting of low-level snowpack in spring occur to bring the river up, the difference of nine feet is quite plausible. Indeed, Lewis writes on April 6, 1806, "from the appearance of a rock near which we had encamped on the 3rd of November last I could judge better of the rise of the water than I could at any point below. I think the flood of this spring has been about 12 feet higher than it was at that time."

It seems evident that the Lewis and Clark Expedition experienced numerous storms with associated cold air aloft from November through March. These conditions, a west-southwest and west-northwest jet stream for much of this time, would have deposited copious amounts of snow in the mountains and foothills of the Columbia River drainage area. Snow greatly delayed the party's crossing of the Rocky Mountains in June.

✳ ✳ ✳

"Multnomah [10] river discharges itself on the S. side of the Columbia 140 miles above the entrance of the latter into the Pacific Ocean, and may be justly esteemed one fourth of that noble river. Capt. C. found that this river had attained it's greatest annual hight and had now fallen about 18 inches."

Meriwether Lewis, April 6, 1806,
near Washougal, Washington.
The Journals of the Lewis & Clark Expedition, Volume 7,
Gary E. Moulton, Editor

On April 2, 1806, Captain Clark departed with six men to explore the lower reaches of the Willamette River. The party passed on the north side of the Columbia River headed downstream toward the ocean, and thus missed this river joining the Columbia River. On their return trip upstream some Native Americans informed them of the river. Clark went to explore and his journey took him as far south as near the present-day site of the St. Johns Bridge across the Willamette River in northwest Portland. Clark's observation that the river had fallen 18 inches from its greatest annual height is interesting.

The Willamette River is subject to tidal fluctuations that are minimized and often eliminated by a strong current. The party's earlier remarks coming up the river regarding a strong current and logs floating down the Columbia

River could very well have been due to an early snowmelt over the drainage of the Willamette River. This river drains an area that is much lower in average elevation and smaller than the Columbia River. An early warm spell had most likely brought down some of the lower and mid-elevation snowpack.

During Clark's excursion up the Willamette River, the weather was mostly fair. His party observed Mt. Jefferson, Mt. Hood, Mt. St. Helens, Mt. Adams and Mt. Rainier. Such sights are rarely visible today because of atmospheric pollution.

✳ ✳ ✳

"this is the most perfectly fair day that we have seen for a Some time. musquetoes troublesome this evening."

Meriwether Lewis, April 6, 1806,
near Washougal, Washington.
The Journals of the Lewis & Clark Expedition, Volume 7,
Gary E. Moulton, Editor

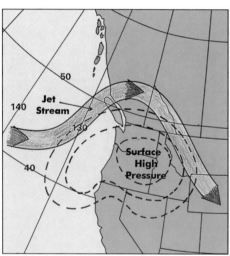

Fig. 3.5 A likely weather pattern in the Pacific Northwest for the period March 30-April 7, 1806 would have an area of surface high pressure (dashed lines) and a jet stream far north into Canada.

Ahhh! Spring in the Pacific Northwest! From March 30 to April 9, the party enjoyed a stretch of wonderful, warm spring weather, and it had been long enough to have brought out the mosquitoes! On April 7, Lewis writes, "the air temperate, birds singing." It must have been a beautiful morning. Obviously a much stronger ridge of high pressure had formed over the area and the jet stream had begun its migration north, if only temporarily (Figure 3.5). Some very light rain occurred on April 3 and 5, but as Lewis mentions on the 4th, "the rains have been very slight."

The party departed their Washougal camp on April 6 and proceeded up river. On April 7, "the day has been fair and weather extreemly pleasant," Lewis wrote. The ridge of high pressure was strengthening and below it a thermal trough[11] was moving up from California and would cause some problems for the party the next day.

✳ ✳ ✳

"The wind blew so violently this morning that we were obliged to unlode our perogues and canoes, soon after which they filled with water."

Meriwether Lewis, April 8, 1806.

"at 7 oClock A.M. the winds Suelded and blew So hard and raised the Waves So emensely high from the N.E."
"The Wind Continued violently hard all day."

William Clark, April 8, 1806,
slightly above today's Rooster Rock State Park.
The Journals of the Lewis & Clark Expedition, Volume 7,
Gary E. Moulton, Editor

When the surface pressure increases east of the Cascade Mountains, and falls west of these mountains, the Columbia River Gorge is the only passage near sea level where wind can travel. A strong east-to-west pressure gradient through this opening can create sustained winds of well over 50 miles per hour with gusts of 75 to 100 mph.[12] The wind direction favors the orientation of the Columbia River. Where the Corps of Discovery was camped, the Columbia River runs from northeast to southwest. These winds are not uncommon during April as a thermal trough sometimes expands north from California into the western valleys of Oregon and Washington, Figure 3.6. This pattern favors that shown in Figure 3.5 with a strong, warm ridge of high pressure aloft.

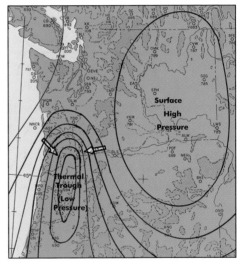

Fig. 3.6 Surface high pressure east of the Cascade Mountains and a thermal trough (low pressure) west of these mountains combine to cause strong east to northeast winds through the Columbia River Gorge.

On April 9, however, the pattern quickly reversed itself. The thermal trough moved east of the Cascade Mountains and the winds at the party's location shifted to westerly, and as Lewis mentions in his weather table on that date, "the wind lulled a little before day, and became high at 11 A.M. continued til dark." His recorded direction was from the west.

Delayed once again by the wind, the party set out up river on April 9. But, the warm ridge of high pressure had weakened and moved east. More storm fronts were pushing east from the Pacific Ocean and quite likely accompanied with colder air aloft. A cold rain occurred during the early morning hours of April 10 and Lewis enters in his journal, "some snow fell on the river hills last night. morning cold, slight sowers through the day." This pattern continued through April 13 with snow falling on the mountains and showers off and on.

❋ ❋ ❋

"I departed and continued my rout with the four canoes along the S. side of the river the wind being too high to pass over to the entrance of the Cruzatts river.[13] *Capt. C. informed me that the wind had detained him several hours a little above Cruzatts river. the wind having lulled in the evening."*

Meriwether Lewis, April 13, 1806,
west of Hood River, Oregon.
The Journals of the Lewis & Clark Expedition, Volume 7,
Gary E. Moulton, Editor

Climatologically, during April winds blowing through the Columbia River Gorge shift from primarily an easterly direction in the winter to a westerly direction during summer. It is also during this time of year that westerly winds can blow very strong, especially after the passage of a surface storm front. High pressure following these fronts can build rapidly into the Pacific Northwest and create a strong pressure gradient through the Columbia River Gorge. (Refer to Figure 1.10) The brief periods of rain with snow falling on the mountains suggest this was occurring during April 1806. This weather regime continued for several days.

❋ ❋ ❋

"even at this place which is merely on the plains of Columbia the climate seems to have changed the air feels dryer and more pure."

Meriwether Lewis, April 17, 1806,
near The Dalles, Wasco County, Oregon.
The Journals of the Lewis & Clark Expedition, Volume 7,
Gary E. Moulton, Editor.

As the party noted when coming down the Columbia River in the fall of 1805, the climate quickly changes from a dry, arid regime near The Dalles to a much wetter regime at the west end of the Columbia River Gorge, Figure 3.7.

Fig. 3.7 Lush vegetation (top) in the west portion of the Columbia River Gorge changes quickly to a dry landscape (bottom) at the east end of this passage through the Cascade Mountains.

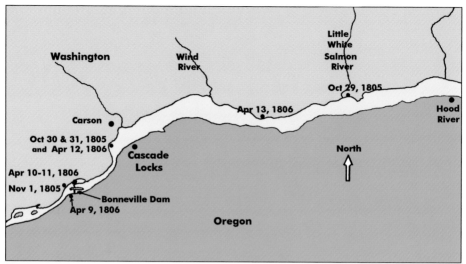

Figure 3.8 The Corps of Discovery campsites for October 29 to November 1, 1805 and April 10-13, 1806 are shown in the above map. Strong winds often disrupted their movement in the Columbia River Gorge.

Figure 3.9 Gusty winds occur on the Columbia River Gorge throughout the year, blowing from a prevailing westerly direction in summer vs. an easterly direction in winter. These winds often hampered movement of the Corps of Discovery but now please windsurfers.

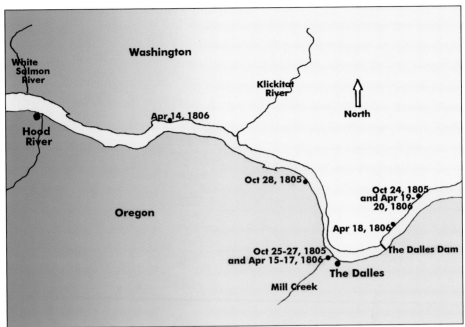

Figure 3.10 The Corps of Discovery campsites for October 24-28, 1805 and for April 14-20, 1806 are shown on the above map.

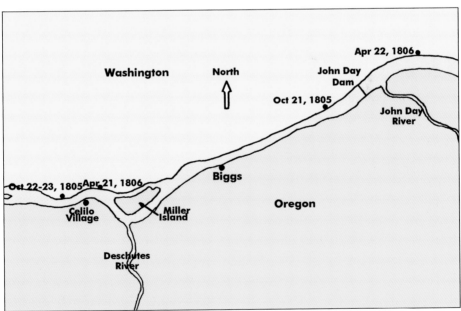

Figure 3.11 Campsites of the Corps of Discovery in the dry area east of the Cascade Mountains, October 21-23, 1805 and April 21-22, 1806 are shown in this Figure.

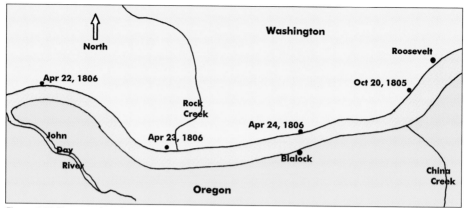

Figure 3.12 The campsites shown are October 20, 1805 and April 22-24, 1806 through the dry, relatively flat area east of the Cascade Mountains.

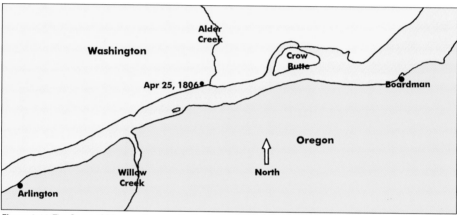

Figure 3.13 The Corps of Discovery's campsite for April 25, 1806 is shown in the above map.

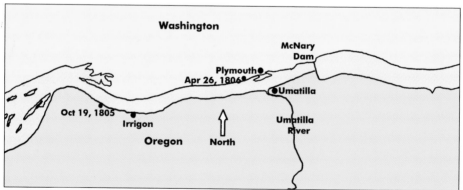

Figure 3.14 The campsites for October 19, 1805 going down the Columbia River and for April 26, 1806 on the return journey are shown in the above Figure.

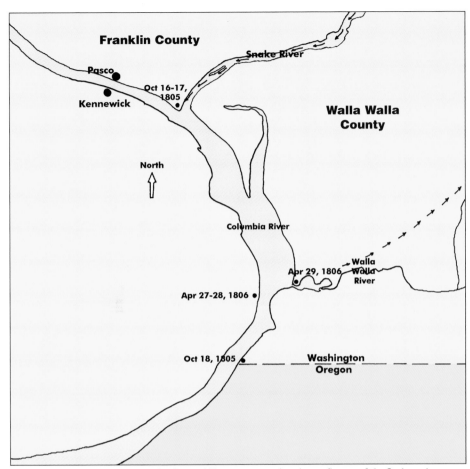

Figure 3.15 Moving downstream the Corps of Discovery camped at the confluence of the Snake and Columbia Rivers. Returning, they camped in southeast Washington near the Walla Walla River.

Figure 3.16 The Corps of Discovery crossed the mouth of the Walla Walla River in southeast Washington on October 18, 1805, and again on their return trip April 29, 1806.

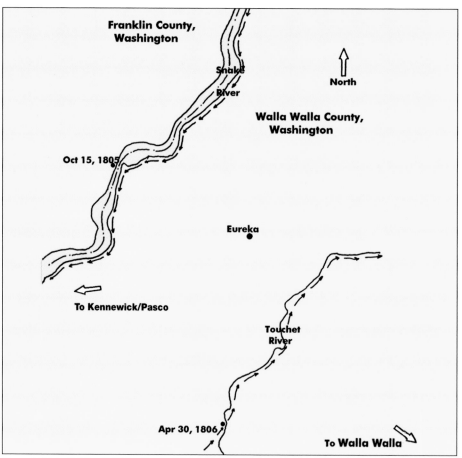

Figure 3.17 In October 1805 the Corps of Discovery traveled down the Snake River but returned next spring via a land route along a portion of the Touchet River in Washington.

Figure 3.18 This marker denotes the Corps of Discovery's campsite May 2, 1806 on Patit Creek northeast of Dayton, Washington on their return trip from the Pacific Ocean (see maps on opposite page).

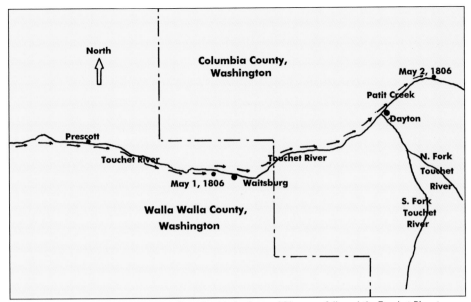

Figure 3.19 On the return trip in the spring of 1806 the Corps of Discovery followed the Touchet River to Patit Creek in southeast Washington.

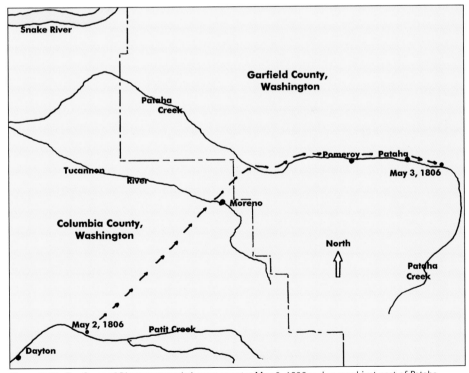

Figure 3.20 The Corps of Discovery traveled cross-country May 3, 1806 and camped just east of Pataha, Washington after enduring a heavy thunderstorm with rain, hail and strong winds.

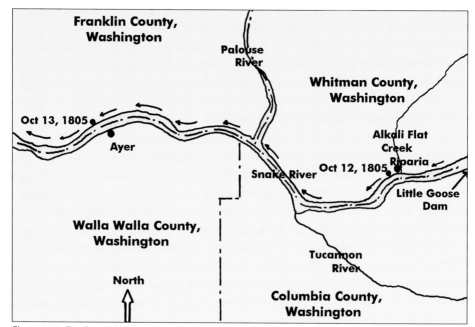

Figure 3.21 The Corps of Discovery traveled down the Snake River in mid-October, often encountering strong west to southwesterly winds.

Figure 3.22 The campsite of October 10, 1805 and again on May 4, 1806 on the Snake River below Clarkston, Washington is now covered with water from the Lower Granite Dam downstream (see map opposite page).

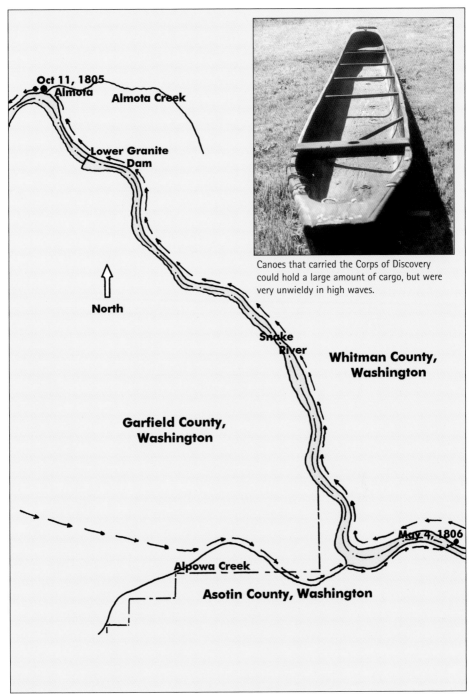

Canoes that carried the Corps of Discovery could hold a large amount of cargo, but were very unwieldy in high waves.

Oct 11, 1805
Almota

Almota Creek

Lower Granite Dam

North

Snake River

Whitman County, Washington

Garfield County, Washington

May 4, 1806

Alpowa Creek

Asotin County, Washington

Figure 3.23 The Corps of Discovery left their camp near Clarkston, Washington on the Snake River and camped October 11, 1805 near Almota. On the return trip they reached the Snake River May 4, 1806 and camped just west of Clarkston, Washington.

The landscape at the eastern end, however, is far different in the spring than in the fall. In spring it is green. Lewis continues his entry for April 17, 1806 with, "the plain is covered with a rich virdure of grass and herbs from four to nine inches high and exhibits a beautifull seen particularly pleasing after having been so long imprisoned in mountains and those almost impenetrably thick forrests of the seacoast." Spring is beautiful east of the Cascade Mountains. But it can also be cold.

Frost is entered in Lewis's weather journal on the mornings of April 20 and 21 while camped just east of The Dalles. Had cherry trees been growing in the area as they are today, it could have been a very cold damaging period. Lewis writes on April 24, "the winds which set from Mount Hood or in a westerly direction are much more cold than those from the opposite quarter. there are now no dews on these plains."

After a brief thundershower during the early morning hours of April 28 the weather cleared. As the party traveled east during the last part of April 1806 across southeast Washington, the Blue Mountains came into view. Lewis enters on April 29, "these mountains are covered with snow at present tho' do not appear high," and again on May 2, "...mountains which appear to be about 25 Ms. distant low yet covered with snow." The party had now passed east of the Columbia River and was traveling along the Touchet River in Walla Walla County, Washington.

Figure 3.24 The Corps of Discovery passed the confluence of the Clearwater River (lower) and Snake River (above) on their journey downstream on October 10, 1805. On the return trip they passed the same location where Clarkston, Washington (right) and Lewiston, Idaho (left) are located today.

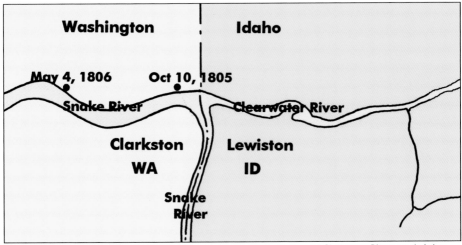

Figure 3.24a The Corps of Discovery passed the confluence of the Snake and Clearwater Rivers on their journey to the Pacific Ocean in the fall of 1805 and on their return trip in the spring of 1806.

✳ ✳ ✳

"here we camped[14] *in small grove of cottonwood tree which in some measure broke the violence of the wind. it rained hailed snowed and blowed with great violence the greater portion of the day. it was fortunate for us that this storm was from the S.W. and of course on our backs. the air was very cold."*

Meriwether Lewis, May 3, 1806,
in southeast Washington.
The Journals of the Lewis & Clark Expedition, Volume 7,
Gary E. Moulton, Editor.

East of the Cascade Mountains, thunderstorms reach their peak during May and June. It appears from the entry on May 3, the party experienced a very strong thunderstorm. Lewis might have thought fortunate, but most thunderstorms east of the Cascade Mountains travel from southwest to northeast. Hail and strong winds frequently accompany them and there have been several tornadoes that have occurred during these two months over the past several years.[15]

This cold upper air trough brought with it a low snow level. Lewis writes on May 4, 1806, "the morning was cold and disagreeable. the S.W. Mountains which appear to be about 15 Ms. above us still continue to become lower they are covered with snow at present nearly to their bases. the evening was cold and disagreeable." Snow down to the foothills of the Blue Mountains the first of May would not bode well for the party when they began their crossing of the Rocky Mountains in June.

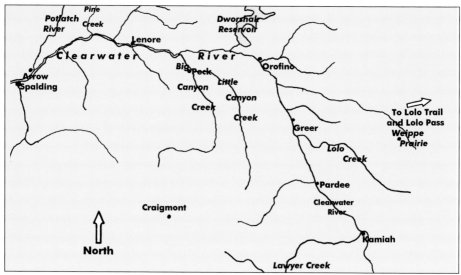

Fig. 3.25 The Corps of Discovery spent time along the Clearwater River in central Idaho both on their journey to the Pacific Ocean and on the return trip to the Rocky Mountains.

On May 4, the party crossed the Snake River. The morning was cold with a hard frost that Lewis measures as 1/8 inch thick. They passed the confluence of the Snake and Clearwater rivers on May 5 (Figures 3.24 and 3.24a) and proceeded up the Clearwater. Showers continued off and on interspersed with periods of fair weather.

✳   ✳   ✳

"The Spurs of the rocky Mountains which were in view from the high plain today were perfectly covered with snow. the Indians inform us that the snow is yet so deep on the mountains that we shall not be able to pass them untill the next full moon about the first of June; others set the time at still a more distant period."

Meriwether Lewis, May 7, 1806,
on the Clearwater River west of Orofino, Idaho
The Journals of the Lewis & Clark Expedition, Volume 7,
Gary E. Moulton, Editor

The westerly jet stream that had plagued them for several months at the mouth of the Columbia River had left its mark in the form of massive snow drifts in the Rocky Mountains. The cold wet spring was heaping even more snow in the mountains, or certainly preventing it from melting. On May 10, the party camped southwest of the town of Kamiah in Lewis County, Idaho. (Figure 3.25) They would remain at this location for a few days.

During the early morning hours of May 10, snow commenced falling and

Figure 3.26 The plains near Weippe Prairie rise 600 to 800 feet above the Clearwater River.

was reported to be 8 inches deep on the plain. In this area, the country near the Clearwater River rises abruptly 600 to 800 feet onto a broad plain. This was just enough of a rise in elevation for precipitation to fall as snow on the plain, but as Lewis mentions on May 10, "I was surprised to find on descending the hills of Commearp Cr.[16] to find that there had been no snow in the bottoms of that stream. it seems that the snow melted in falling and decended here in rain while it snowed on the plains." On the morning of May 11, the rain and snow ceased, but hunters returning to camp reported it still remained on the plains. Winter was certainly not over for the Corps of Discovery.

On May 13, the Corps of Discovery moved their camp to near the present-day town of Kamiah. On May 14 a permanent camp was established on the east bank of the Clearwater River about two miles below the mouth of Lawyer Creek. They would remain at this location until June 10, at which time they would attempt to cross the Rocky Mountains. They were greeted with a few days of fair weather.

September 15-22, 1805 - The Corps of Discovery camped at various locations in the Central Idaho Mountains sometimes along the Lolo Trail. The party was often separated with different campsites on some days. Captain Clark entered Weippe Prairie on September 20, 1805 and descended to the Clearwater River on September 21. Captain Lewis descended into Weippe Prairie on September 22 and was joined there by Captain Clark. Their camp that night was on Jim Ford Creek in Weippe Prairie.

September 23, 1805 - About one mile southwest of Weippe, Clearwater County, Idaho.

September 24-25, 1805 - About a mile above Orofino, Clearwater County, Idaho, perhaps on what is now China Island.

September 26-October 7, 1805 - At what was called "Canoe Camp" about 5 miles west of Orofino, Clearwater County, Idaho on the south bank of the Clearwater River.

October 8-9, 1805 - Below the confluence of the Potlatch and Clearwater Rivers a few miles from Spalding, Idaho.

October 10, 1805 - Slightly below the confluence of the Snake and Clearwater Rivers on the north side.

Table 3.1 This table indicates the locations where the Corps of Discovery camped after crossing the Rocky Mountains into Idaho until October 10, 1805. (Locations from Moulton.).

✳ ✳ ✳

It rained the greater part of last night and this morning until 8 Ock. it rained
moderately the greater part of the day and snowed as usual on the plain.

Meriwether Lewis, May 17, 1806.

"At the distance of 18 miles from the river and on the eastern border
of the high Plain the rocky Mountain Commences and presents us with
Winter here we have summer, Spring and Winter in the Short space
of twenty or thirty miles."

William Clark, May 18, 1806,
near Kamiah, Idaho.
The Journals of the Lewis & Clark Expedition, Volume 7,
Gary E. Moulton, Editor.

Changes of climate are certainly to be found where there are abrupt changes in elevation. Lewis remarked that the vegetation on the plains was at least 15 to 20 days behind that found down next to the river near Kamiah, Idaho. They often sweltered in the heat at their camp while hunters reported snow still not melted on the higher plains.

Perhaps it was another cold, upper-level low-pressure area that kept hanging around because the rain in the valley and snow on the plains continued intermittently through the morning of May 21. A fine, cold morning greeted the party on May 22 and 23. Clark notes on May 23 that hunters returning from the plains reported, "the high lands are very cold with snow which has fallen for every day or night for Several past."

May 5, 1806 - On the Clearwater River, in the vicinity of Arrow, Idaho, just below the confluence of the Potlatch River ("Colters Creek") and the Clearwater River.
May 6, 1806 - On the Clearwater River estimated to be near or slightly below the mouth of Pine Creek.
May 7, 1806 - Probably south of Peck, Idaho on the east side of Big Canyon Creek.
May 8, 1806 - A few miles west or southwest of Orofino.
May 9, 1806 - Slightly southwest of Orofino.
May 10-12, 1806 - On Lawyer Creek southwest of Kamiah.
May 13, 1806 - Near the present Kamiah, Idaho railroad depot.
May 14-June 9, 1806 - On the east bank of the Clearwater River just below the town of Kamiah and about two miles below the mouth of Lawyer Creek.
June 10-14, 1806 - On Weippe Prairie, Clearwater County, Idaho.
June 15, 1806 - On Eldorado Creek, near the mouth of Lunch Creek, Idaho County, Idaho.
June 16, 1806 - At Horsesteak Meadow on Hungery Creek, Idaho County, Idaho.
June 17, 1806 - On the south side of Hungery Creek.
June 18-20, 1806 - On Eldorado Creek, at the mouth of Dollar Creek, Idaho County, Idaho.
June 21-23, 1806 - On Weippe Prairie.
June 24, 1806 - On Eldorado Creek, at the mouth of Dollar Creek, Idaho County, Idaho.
June 25, 1806 - Probably near where the main party camped on September 19, 1805 on a small creek emptying into Hungery Creek.
June 27, 1806 - On Bald Mountain, Idaho County, Idaho.
June 28, 1806 - Near Powell Junction a few miles north of the current Powell Ranger Station.
June 29, 1806 - Lolo Hot Springs, Missoula County, Montana.

Table 3.2 This table indicates the approximate locations of where the Corps of Discovery camped from early May, 1806 until they crossed into Montana in late June. (Locations from Moulton.)

Fig. 3.27 The Weippe Prairie area looks much the same today as it did when the Corps of Discovery camped here in September 1805 and in June 1806.

Another couple of days of clear weather allowed the party to dry out. But the respite was short. On May 25, Lewis writes, "It rained the greater part of last night and continued until 6 A.M. our grass tent is impervious to the rain." Weather once more became disagreeable with frequent showers and thunder-showers until the afternoon of June 1. On May 31, however, another remark by Meriwether Lewis attests to the extent of the winter snow when he remarks about the river, "it rose Eighteen inches and is now as high as any marks of it's having been for several years past."

A shower or two occurred the first few days of June, but for the most part it was fair. On June 8, Lewis enters in his journal, "one of the indians informed us that we could not pass the mountains untill the full of the next moon or about the first of July, that if we attempted it sooner our horses would be at least three days travel without food on the top of the mountain. this information is disagreeable inasmuch as it causes some doubt as to the time at which it will be most proper for us to set out." The party was getting anxious to leave. On June 9, Lewis wrote, "the river has been falling for several days and is now lower by six feet than it has been; this we view as a strong evidence that the great body of snow has left the mountains..." The party was thinking as this author thinks: "When I am to ready leave a place, I want to leave, and I leave." On June 10, they left their camp near Kamiah and proceeded northeast across Lolo Creek towards Weippe Prairie (Figure 3.27).

The party camped on Weippe Prairie for 5 days. During that time the weather seemed quite typical for spring in central Idaho. They had warm days and cool nights and were visited by thunder, lightning and rain on June 12. A hard rain, however, commenced as they left this camp and proceeded to cross the Rocky Mountains which loomed ahead, covered with snow.

✳ ✳ ✳

"the snow has increased in quantity so much that the greater part of our rout this evening, was over the snow which has become sufficiently firm to bear our horshes, otherwise it would have been impossible for us to proceed as it lay in immence masses in some places 8 or ten feet deep."

Meriwether Lewis, June 16, 1806,
along Hungery Creek, Idaho County, Idaho.
The Journals of the Lewis & Clark Expedition, Volume 8,
Gary E. Moulton, Editor

It was indeed a very heavy snowfall in the Rocky Mountains of Idaho. As the party progressed onward and upward, Lewis's entry for June 17 was, "this hill or reather mountain we ascended about 3 miles when we found ourselves invelloped in snow from 12 to 15 feet deep even on the south sides of the hills with the fairest exposure to the sun." The party turned back. The weather, this time snow, had won another hand.[17] To add to their woes, a cold rain was falling and the melting snow made every creek a rushing torrent, each difficult to cross.

✳ ✳ ✳

"this hill or reather mountain we ascended about 3 miles when we found ourselves invelloped in snow from 12 to 15 feet deep even on the south sides of the hills with the fairest exposure to the sun; here was winter with all it's rigors; the air was cold, my hands and feet were benumbed."

Meriwether Lewis, June 17, 1806,
in the mountains of central Idaho north of the Lochsa River.
The Journals of the Lewis & Clark Expedition, Volume 8,
Gary E. Moulton, Editor

✳ ✳ ✳

"...but it appeared to me somewhat extraordinary, to be travelling over snow six or eight feet deep in the latter end of June."[18]

Patrick Gass, June 27, 1806
On Springhill or Spring Mountain, Idaho
The Journals of the Lewis & Clark Expedition, Volume 10
Gary E. Moulton, Editor

The deep snow forced the party to return to Weippe Prairie where they remained for a few days. On June 24, the party made another attempt to cross the Rocky Mountains. They found that the snow had subsided by about 4 feet. For the most part, during the last leg of their journey up and over the Rocky Mountains, the weather was for once not a factor. The freezing level had risen and light rain fell on the party occasionally with one thunderstorm. They crossed into Montana on June 29, 1806.

1. Moulton indicates they passed the Long Narrows, part of The Dalles of the Columbia River, on October 25, 1805.

2. For simplicity the period includes the first few days of November and the last few days of March. These two periods include the time the party spent on the lower Columbia River from Portland, Oregon to the Pacific Ocean in November 1805 and their return up the river in late March 1806. 2004 was a leap year.

3. Lewis records snow on three days during the latter part of January, but no rain.

4. Lewis records snow on February 2, 1806, but no rain.

5. For the months of January, February and March, Lewis has a weather entry at sunrise and one at 4 PM. For November and December, there is only one entry and no indication as to when that observation was made.

6. A trace of precipitation indicates that some form of precipitation fell during the day, but the water equivalent was less than 0.01 inch.

7. These averages are from the Western Regional Climate Center and are for the total period the station has been in operation since 1953.

8. The Chah-wah-na-hi-ooks River is the Lewis River in southwest Washington.

9. Conversation with Charles Orwig, Hydrologist, Northwest River Forecast Center.

10. The Multnomah is the Willamette River.

11. See Glossary for an explanation of the thermal trough.

12. When a weather station was in operation at Crown Point, elevation 650 feet, just to the west of Rooster Rock State Park, wind gusts of over 100 mph were recorded.

13. The Cruzatts River is the Wind River in Skamania County, Washington.

14. In Garfield County, Washington on Pataha Creek east of Pataha.

15. On July 9, 1995 a severe thunderstorm developed in the afternoon near Bend, Oregon. It moved east-northeastward through Condon & Hermiston, Oregon into southeast Washington. The storm caused millions of dollars in damage to wheat fields and car dealerships, producing strong gusty winds and hail the size of golf balls and baseballs.

16. Commearp Creek is Lawyer Creek in Lewis County Idaho, southwest of Kamiah.

17. The author visited the Lolo Pass area on June 17, 2003. The area was virtually free of snow except for some remaining on the higher peaks. It is normally gone from the area by late June.

18. Extraordinary indeed! Conversation with National Resources Conservation Service individuals at Portland, Oregon and Boise, Idaho revealed average snow depths in the area June 1 to be 5 inches at 5,000 feet; 1-2 feet at 5,500 feet; 3-4 feet at 6,000 feet. Only in June 1997 did recorded values approach those the Corps of Discovery experienced.

Epilogue

* * *

*"last evening the indians entertained us with seting the fir trees on fire.
they have a great number of dry lims near their bodies which when set
on fire creates a very suddon and immence blaze from the bottom to top
of those tall trees. They are a beatiful object in this situation at night.
this exhibition reminded me of a display of fireworks.
The natives told us that their object in seting those trees on fire
was to bring fair weather for our journey."*

Meriwether Lewis, June 25, 1806,
on El Dorado Creek, Idaho County, Idaho.
The Journals of the Lewis & Clark Expedition, Volume 8,
Gary E. Moulton, Editor

Perhaps the Corps of Discovery could have used a few more burning trees in their journey from the Rocky Mountains to the Pacific Ocean, their winter at the mouth of the Columbia River and their return back to the Rocky Mountains. Mother Nature hurled at them just about everything she had to offer—thunderstorms, rain, wind, hail, snow, cold and even episodes of hot weather. But was the weather then very different from today's? The author thinks naught, except for one item.

Descending the Rocky Mountains in September, their first encounter was with an early snowstorm, but not unusual for the northern Rocky Mountains. They enjoyed some superb fall weather in late September and early October which is quite common for eastern Washington and western Idaho. Fall began slowly with a few rainstorms as they paddled down the Columbia River.

For the winter, however, precipitation did appear to be above normal for coastal areas of the Pacific Northwest, but it may not have been a record. It must be remembered, however, that this was not the type of winter that the party was used to. During the winters they were accustomed to, the skies did not open up for days and days drenching the party with rain and no sunshine. They could remember winters with cold and snow, which they did receive for two weeks at Fort Clatsop.

That cold spell, however, was somewhat unprecedented for the Pacific

Northwest, at least today. Temperatures in the teens along the coastal strip, where the ocean has a great influence, would likely translate into single-digit numbers for western valleys of Washington and Oregon and far below zero for the area east of the Cascade Mountains. The length of the cold spell was also far longer than what is normal for the Pacific Northwest. Today, these often last for just a few days along the coast, perhaps a week in the western valleys and two weeks east of the Cascade Mountains. The party got a good taste of winter while camped at Fort Clatsop. One can only wonder how well they would have fared had they camped farther inland from the Pacific Ocean. They complained of the rain, but it very well could have been their saving grace.

And what else can be said about the depth of the snow in their aborted and delayed trip across the Rocky Mountains. While they were at Fort Clatsop when snow was visible on Saddle Mountain many days and those mornings when they awoke to find a dusting of wet snow certainly indicates the freezing level was often 1,000 to 2,000 feet. A westerly jet stream must have pounded the Cascade Mountains and Rocky Mountains with snowstorm after snowstorm during the winter of 1805/1806. The party encountered these deep drifts well into the month of June. They endured and reached St. Louis safely, but weather had played a major role in their journey. Yes, many times that weather was DISAGREEABLE!

When winds subside, the Columbia River can become quite calm as shown in the area near Cathlamet, Washington looking south. Rain showers, however, can still prevail.

Bibliography

BOOKS

Ahrens, C. Donald (2001) Third Printing; *Essentials of Meteorology An Invitation to the Atmosphere*; Wadsworth Group, a Division of Thompson Learning Inc.; contact Brooks/Cole, Pacific Grove, CA.

(The) Climate of Oregon, Climate Zone 6, North Central Area; Special Report 918, May 1993; Agricultural Experiment Station, Oregon State University.

Fifer, Barbara and Vicky Soderberg, (2001 Second Edition), *Along the Trail with Lewis and Clark*, Farcountry Press, Helena, Montana

Glickman, Todd S. (2000) 2nd Edition, *Glossary of Meteorology*, American Meteorological Society, Boston, Massachusetts.

Jackson, Donald (1978); *Letters of the Lewis and Clark Expedition with Related Documents 1783-1854;* Second Edition, with Additional Documents and Notes; Edited by Donald Jackson; Volume 1; University of Illinois Press; Urbana and Chicago.

(The) Journals of Patrick Gass, Member of the Lewis and Clark Expedition, (1997), Edited and annotated by Carol Lynn MacGregor, Mountain Press Publishing company, Missoula, Montana.

Lang, H.O., *History of the Willamette Valley*, together with Personal Reminiscences of Its Early Pioneers., (1885), published by Himes & Lang, Portland, Oregon, Geo. H. Himes, Book and Job Printer.

McInerney, Mark A. (1996), National Weather Service Office Astoria, Oregon, *Climate of Astoria, Oregon*, NOAA Technical Memorandum NWS WR-236.

Miller, George R., (2002) *Pacific Northwest Weather: But My Barometer Says Fair*, Amato Publications Inc., Portland, Oregon.

Moulton, Gary E., Editor, (1999) Fourth Printing, *The Journals of the Lewis & Clark Expedition*, Volume 5, University of Nebraska Press, Lincoln, Nebraska.

Moulton, Gary E., Editor, (1998) Third Printing, *The Journals of the Lewis & Clark Expedition*, Volume 6, University of Nebraska Press, Lincoln, Nebraska.

Moulton, Gary E., Editor, (1998) Second Printing, *The Journals of the Lewis & Clark Expedition*, Volume 7, University of Nebraska Press, Lincoln, Nebraska.

Moulton, Gary E., Editor, (2000) Third Printing, *The Journals of the Lewis & Clark Expedition*, Volume 8, University of Nebraska Press, Lincoln, Nebraska.

Moulton, Gary E., Editor, (1999) Third Printing, *The Journals of the Lewis & Clark Expedition*, Volume 9, University of Nebraska Press, Lincoln, Nebraska.

Moulton, Gary E., Editor, (1998) Second Printing, *The Journals of the Lewis & Clark Expedition*, Volume 10, University of Nebraska Press, Lincoln, Nebraska.

Moulton, Gary E., Editor, (1998) Second Printing, *The Journals of the Lewis & Clark Expedition*, Volume 11, University of Nebraska Press, Lincoln, Nebraska.

Moulton, Gary E., Editor, (2002) First Paperback Printing, *The Definitive Journals of Lewis & Clark, Over the Rockies to St. Louis, Volume 8*, University of Nebraska Press, Lincoln, Nebraska.

Reports to the Nation, Spring 1994, A publication of the University Corporation for Atmospheric Research pursuant to National Oceanic and Atmospheric Administration Award No. NA27GPO232-01.

Rockey, Clinton C. D., National Weather Service Forecast Office Portland, Oregon (1999), *Climate of Portland, Oregon*, NOAA technical Memorandum NWS WR-239, First Revision.

Taylor, George H., Raymond R. Hatton, (1999), *The Oregon Weather Book, A State of Extremes*, Oregon State University Press, Corvalis, Oregon.

Ziak, Rex, (2002), *In Full View*, Moffit House Press, Astoria, Oregon.

MANUSCRIPTS AND PERIODICALS

Koch, Roy W. and Austin R. Fisher, *Effects of Inter-annual and Decadal-scale Variability on Winter and Spring Streamflow in western Oregon and Washington*; Department of Civil Engineering Sciences, Portland State University

Quinn, W.H. and V.T. Neal, (1992), *The Historical Record of El Nino Events*, Reprinted from "Climate Since A.D. 1500," edited by R.S. Bradley and P.D. Jones, Routledge London.

Glossary

Canoe Camp: Where the Lewis and Clark Expedition camped on the Clearwater River in Idaho about 5 miles west of Orofino from September 26 to October 6, 1805.

Cold Low Aloft: An area of cold, unstable air aloft, generally divorced from the westerly jet stream, that usually drifts slowly from west to east.

Downcanyon Winds: Nocturnal winds that begin moving down a slope into a canyon or valley after sunset as radiation cools the earth and subsequently the air in contact with it.

El Niño: A warming of the central and eastern tropical Pacific Ocean near the equator due to weakening or reversal of the northeast and southeast trade winds.

Fair: In earlier forecast wording, generally speaking, the absence of rain and cloudiness that may obstruct the sun's radiation. The term is no longer used by the National Weather Service.

Freezing Level: The level in the atmosphere where the free air temperature lowers to 32° Fahrenheit or 0° Celsius.

Front: In meteorological terminology, the boundary between two air masses with different qualities. A warm front is warm air advancing displacing cold air; a cold front is cold air advancing displacing warm air.

Isobar: A line along which the pressure is the same.

Jet Stream: A fast-moving band or ribbon of air from 20,000 to 40,000 feet in the middle latitudes. Speeds often reach 175 to 200 miles per hour. Storms and their associated frontal systems move along this band of air.

Point Ellice: This point of land was called several names by the expedition. Point Distress, Stormey Point, Blustering Point. Today it is where the Astoria Bridge ends in Washington.

Pressure Gradient: The difference in surface air pressure between two points. Large differences are often referred to as a strong pressure gradient.

Showers: Rain of usually short duration, often heavy, that is often interspersed with sunny periods or partly cloudy weather for short intervals.

Snow Level: The lowest layer in the atmosphere where snow is falling before it melts. This level can occur 1,000 to 1,500 feet below the actual freezing level.

Thermal Trough: An extension northward of the heat or thermal low that forms over the southwest portion of the United States from April through October. Certain atmospheric conditions bring this feature north. Strong east winds can occur with this weather event, west of Cascade Mountains..

Unstable Atmosphere: An air mass consisting of relatively warm air near the surface and much cooler air aloft. As a bubble of air rises, if it is warmer than the surrounding air, it will continue to rise.

Upcanyon Winds: Winds that begin moving up a slope or a canyon as the sun's radiation heats the earth and subsequently the air in contact with it.

Upper-level Trough: In the middle and upper atmosphere, an area of lower pressure associated with cooler air.

Wind Chill: An apparent temperature that relates to how cold a person "feels." Wind chill is derived from the free air temperature and the wind speed.

Index

Adams Point (See Point Adams)

Alaska 8, 36

Alder Creek 56

Aldrich Point 44, 46

Alkali Flat Creek 60

Almota 61

Almota Creek 61

Alpowa Creek 61

Altoona, Oregon 38

arctic air 5, 36-39

Arlington, Oregon 12, 56

Arrow, Idaho 64, 66

Astoria, Oregon 6, 15, 17, 21, 23, 24, 27, 29, 33, 37, 42-45

atmosphere 9, 18, 23, 29, 36, 39, 50

Ayer, Washington 11, 60

Baker Bay 21, 33

barometer 23

Beacon Rock 48

Bend, Oregon 69

Big Canyon Creek 64, 66

Biggs, Oregon 55

Blalock, Oregon 56

Blue Mountains 62, 63

Boardman, Oregon 56

Bonneville Dam 15, 42, 54

British Columbia 27

Brookfield, Oregon 38

Brownsmead, Oregon 44

California 6, 22, 50, 51

calm 15, 20, 23

Canada 8, 11, 36, 47

Canoe Camp 5, 10, 11, 65

Cape Disappointment 21

Cape Horn 45

Carson, Washington 54

Cascade Locks, Oregon 54

Cascade Mountains 12-14, 24, 30, 31, 34, 38, 39, 51, 53, 55, 56, 62, 63, 71

Carson, Washington 54

Cascade Locks, Oregon 54

Cathlamet, Washington 16, 44

Celilo Village, Oregon 55

Chah-wah-na-hi-ooks River
    (See Lewis River)

China Creek 56

Chinook Point, Washington 20, 21, 24

Christmas 31

cirrostratus 16, 35

Clarkston, Washington 60-63

Clatskanie, Oregon 45, 46

Clearwater County, Idaho 65, 66

Clearwater River 5, 10, 11, 62-66

clear, clearing 12, 15, 18, 19, 23, 24, 26, 34, 37, 38, 43, 46, 48, 62, 67

climate 10, 12, 13, 24, 52, 66

clouds, cloudiness, cloudy 14-16, 23, 24, 32, 35, 37, 39, 40, 42, 43

Coast Range Mountains 22, 24, 30, 32

cold front 11, 12

Columbia River 5, 12, 13, 15-22, 24-26, 30, 33, 34, 40, 41, 43-53, 56, 57, 62, 64, 69, 70; average flow of 48

Columbia River Bar 41

Columbia River Gorge 5, 12-14, 39, 51-54

Columbus Day Storm 21-23, 42

Commearp Creek (See Lawyer Creek)

Condon, Oregon 69

Cowlitz River 16, 46

Craigmont, Idaho 64

Crow Butte 56

Crown Point, Oregon 69

Cruzatts River (See Wind River)

Dayton, Washington 58, 59

Deer Island 46, 47

Deschutes River 55

downcanyon winds 10, 11

Drewyer (See Drouillard, George)

Drouillard, George

Dworshak Reservoir 64

El Nino 8, 19, 45

Eureka, Washington 58

fetch 16, 17

fog 15

Fort Canby State Park 20, 21

Fort Clatsop 5, 21, 27-32, 34, 35, 38-40, 43,
     45, 70, 71

Fort Mandan 8, 36, 39

freezing level 14, 18, 28, 40, 69, 71

freezing rain 38, 42

frost 23, 27, 28, 33-35, 41, 62, 64

Fujita Tornado Scale 29

Gass, Patrick 10, 16, 21-23, 26, 28, 29, 34,
     38, 42, 46, 47, 68

Government Island 47, 48

Gray's Bay 16, 17, 44

Gree, Idaho 64

Gulf of California 9

Gulf of Mexico 9

hail 18, 19, 26, 29, 30, 32, 39, 41, 59, 63, 69,
     70

Hayden Island 47, 48

Hermiston, Oregon 69

high-pressure 11, 14-16, 20, 24, 26, 35, 50-52

Hood River, Oregon 13, 52, 54, 55

Hungery Creek 66, 68

ice, icicles 5, 36, 37

ice pellets 18

Idaho 8, 9, 11, 12, 35, 39, 47, 63, 70

Indian Summer 15, 19

Irrigon, Oregon 56

isobar 14, 17, 26

jet stream 8, 11, 14, 16-18, 20-25, 28, 30,
     34-36, 39, 40, 49, 50, 64, 71

John Day Dam 55

John Day River 55, 56

Juno 41

Kalama River 15, 46

Kalama, Washington 15

Kamiah, Idaho 64-67

Kelso, Washington 46

Kennewick, Washington 57, 58

Klickitat River 55

Lawyer Creek 64-66, 69

Lenore, Idaho 64

LePage, Jean Baptiste 38

Lewis and Clark River 38, 42

Lewis County, Idaho 64

Lewis River 47, 69

Lewiston, Idaho 10, 62, 63

lightning 7, 9, 18, 26, 30, 31, 68

Little Canyon Creek 64

Little Goose Dam 60

Little White Salmon River 54

Lochasa River 68

Lolo Creek 64, 67

Lolo Pass 9, 64, 69

Lolo Trail 8, 9, 64, 69

Long Beach Peninsula 31

Long Beach, Washington 29

Longview, Washington 45, 46

Lower Granite Dam 60, 61

low-pressure 9, 11, 14, 16, 17, 22, 25, 26, 28, 30, 51, 66

Mandans 8

McNary Dam 56

Mill Creek, Oregon 12, 55

Miller Island 55

Montana 8, 47, 66

Moon Creek, Idaho County, Idaho 8

Moreno, Washington 59

Mount Adams 50

Mount Hood 48, 50, 62

Mount Jefferson 50

Mount Rainier 50

Mount St. Helens 48, 50

Multnomah Channel 47

Multnomah County, Oregon 15

Multnomah River (See Willamette River)

Naselle, Washington 42

National Resources Conservation Service 69

National Weather Service 4, 44

Nehalem River 40

Netul River (See Lewis and Clark River)

Nevada 47

New Archangel (Sitka, Alaska) 41

Newport, Oregon 42

North Dakota 8, 36

Ordway, John 13, 18, 21, 22, 34, 38

Oregon 6, 11-13, 15, 21, 22, 29, 38, 39, 42, 44-47, 51, 54-56, 71

Orofino, Idaho 10, 64-66

Oysterville, Washington 29

Pacific County, Washington 21, 29

Pacific Ocean 6, 14, 17, 20-24, 34, 35, 37, 45, 49, 52, 69, 70

Palouse River 60

Pardee, Idaho 64

Pasco, Washington 57, 58

Pataha, Washington 59, 69

Pataha Creek 59, 69

Patit Creek 58, 59

Peck, Idaho 64, 66

Point Adams, Oregon 21, 38

Point Ellice, Washington 17, 18, 20, 21, 24

Point Chinook, Washington (See Chinook Point)

Pomeroy, Washington 59

Portland, Oregon 6, 15, 23, 24, 49, 69

Potlatch River 64-66

precipitation 12, 15, 17, 18, 31, 32, 34, 42, 44, 45, 49, 65, 70

Prescott, Washington 59

pressure 22, 23, 40, 42, 51

pressure gradient 12, 14, 22, 23, 51

Pryor, Nathaniel Hale 38

Puget Island 38, 44

radiation 10, 11

Quinn, William H 19

Rainier, Oregon 46

Riparia, Washington 60

Rock Creek 56

Rocky Mountains 5, 6, 8, 9, 30, 41, 43, 49, 63-66, 68-71

Roosevelt, Washington 12, 56

Rooster Rock State Park 15, 51, 69

Saddle Mountain, Oregon 18, 19, 42, 71

Sandy River 48

Sauvie Island 47

Seaside, Oregon 27-29

showers, showery 19, 26, 30-32, 41, 52, 64, 67

Skamakowa, Washington 16, 44

Snake River 11, 57-65

snow level 30, 39, 63, 67-69

snowmelt 46, 48, 50

snowpack, snowdrift, snowfall 39, 40,
   48-50, 64, 68

Spalding, Idaho 64, 65

squall 32

St. Helens, Oregon 47

St. Johns Bridge 47, 49

storm 6, 8, 9, 13, 15-18, 21-23, 25, 26, 28,
   30, 32, 33, 35, 39-41, 46, 47, 49

storm front 11, 17, 46, 52

storm, January 9, 1880 25

stratus clouds 15

sun, sunny, sunshine 7, 15, 20, 24, 26, 28,
   32-36, 39, 41, 43, 46

swells 16, 17

temperature 9, 23, 24, 35-39, 71

Tenasillahe Island 44

The Dalles Dam 55

The Dalles, Oregon 6, 12, 13, 23, 24, 26, 38,
   39, 48, 52, 55, 62, 69

thermal trough 50, 51

thermometer 7, 35, 37

Thomas Jefferson 7

thunder, thundershower, thunderstorm 7, 9,
   10, 18, 19, 26, 29-31, 33, 59, 62, 63, 67,
   68, 70

Tillamook Head 34

Tomahawk Island 48

Tongue Point, Oregon 21, 25, 43, 45

tornado 29, 63

Touchet River 58, 59, 62

trough 9, 17-19, 25, 28, 30, 37, 39, 41, 51, 63

Tucannon River 59, 60

typhoon 23

Typhoon Freda 23

Umatilla, Oregon 56

Umatilla River 56

unstable 9, 10, 18, 29, 39, 41

upcanyon winds 10, 11

Utah 47

Vancouver, Washington 47, 48

Viento, Oregon 39

Wahkiakum County, Washington 16

Waitsburg, Washington 59

Walla Walla River 57

Walla Walla, Washington 6, 57, 58

Washington 11-13, 15, 21, 22, 27, 29, 39,
   44-47, 51, 54-56, 63, 70, 71

Washougal River 48

Washougal, Washington 48-50

watershed 40

waves 5, 14, 16, 17, 19, 25, 26, 40, 51, 61

Weippe, Idaho 9, 65

Weippe Prairie 64-69

Western Regional Climate Center 69

White Salmon River 55

White Salmon, Washington 13

Whitehouse, Joseph 12, 14, 17, 21, 22, 26,
   34, 38, 47

Willamette River 47, 49, 50, 69

Willamette Valley 39

Willow Creek 56

wind chill 19

Wind River 52, 54, 69

windsurfers 14, 54

Winter 1861-62 39

Winter 1884-85 39

Woodland, Washington 15, 47

Wyoming 47

Young's Bay 27

LEWIS & CLARK'S **NORTHWEST JOURNEY**

About the Author

Since retiring from the national Weather Service after 35 years George Miller has continued his interest in weather. He has taught classes in meteorology and climatology at Portland State University, Marylhurst University and Clackamas Community College. His first book, *Pacific Northwest Weather: But My Barometer Says Fair* is used as a textbook in one of the classes he teaches. He has examined countless documents looking for clues as to past weather in the Pacific Northwest. The meticulous records kept by several members of the Corps of Discovery give a brief glimpse of past weather in this area.

HIKING MT. HOOD NATIONAL FOREST
By Marcia Sinclair

Oregon has been blessed with great natural beauty, one of its highlights is spectacular Mt. Hood and surrounding Mt. Hood National Forest. Less than one hour from downtown Portland, this natural wonder is a popular hiking destination. Marcia covers numerous hikes, what you can expect on each trail, including historical information and highlighting the flora and fauna you will experience along the way. 6 x 9 inches, 5 1/2 x 8 1/2, 130 pages.

SB: $19.95   **ISBN: 1-57188-271-5**

RAPTORS OF THE PACIFIC NORTHWEST
Thomas Bosakowski and Dwight G. Smith

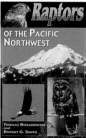

Over the centuries, raptors have become both symbolic and metaphor for beauty, courage, swiftness, and above all, ferocity. In the U.S., raptors have been displayed as an emblem of strength, freedom, and power. *Raptors of the Northwest* features the following information on 35 species found throughout the Pacific Northwest: range; life history; behavior; conservation status; habitat requirements; nesting; eggs and young; hunting behavior and diet; territory and density; survey methods; conservation and management. 6 x 9 inches, 136 pages.

SB: $19.95   **ISBN: 1-57188-236-7**

50 HIKES FOR EASTERN WASHINGTON'S HIGHEST MOUNTAINS
James P. Johnson

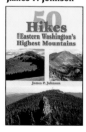

Visit backcountry that's rarely visited, and see stunning views rarely seen!
You don't have to be a world-class mountaineer to reach Eastern Washington's highest summits. They can be climbed without use of special gear or skills, and all can be reached on a day-hike. With a wide variety of difficulty, you can choose peaks that match your level of hiking expertise. This book features: the 50 highest mountains of Eastern Washington; color photos and trail maps for each mountain; detailed descriptions for finding and hiking each mountain; view descriptions for the top of each summit. 6 x 9 inches, 119 pages.

SB: $14.95   **ISBN: 1-57188-296-0**

COLUMBIA RIVER: END OF THE LEWIS AND CLARK TRAIL
Bryan Penttila

Many of us are familiar with the story of Lewis and Clark as they crossed the country in search of the Pacific Ocean, but what of the people who inhabited the region before and after their adventure? The Pacific Northwest has a rich and fascinating history, especially along the mighty Columbia River near Astoria, Oregon. Through text and over 100 historical photographs, Penttila shares the tough everyday lives and extraordinary events of the Native inhabitants and the early settlers. Whether you're from the Pacific Northwest or not, you will find this book very difficult to put down. 8 1/2 x 11 inches, 88 pages.

SB: $15.95   **ISBN: 1-57188-302-9**

PACIFIC NORTHWEST WEATHER
George R. Miller

The climate of the Pacific Northwest is as broad and varied as is found anywhere in the world—from dry eastern sections to cool and wet western regions. *Pacific Northwest Weather* explores the reasons for this, offering an in-depth look into those peculiarities specific to Pacific Northwest weather. Written and designed for the layperson, as well as a basic text in meteorology, this book explains how weather occurs on a global scale down to the small-scale way in which your campfire smoke drifts. With interesting references to past storms, like the infamous Columbus Day storm, and weather patterns that cause heat waves and ice storms, this book has much to offer anyone interested in the weather. 8 1/2 x 11 inches, 170 pages.

SB: $25.00   **ISBN: 1-57188-235-9**

COLUMBIA GORGE HIKES
Don and Roberta Lowe

Oregon's Columbia Gorge is one of the most gorgeous spots on the planet. Don and Roberta Lowe have been hiking and photographing the Gorge for a combined 85 years, in this book they share the beauty that abounds in this region. Forty-two hikes covered, including hike length, elevation gain, high point, time needed, when open, and what you can expect to find along the way. 8 1/2 x 11 inches, 80 pages.

SB: $19.95   **ISBN: 1-57188-203-0**

ASK FOR THESE BOOKS AT YOUR LOCAL BOOK STORE. IF UNAVAILABLE, CALL TOLL FREE 1-800-541-9498 (Pacific time 8-5), FAX 503-653-2766, OR ORDER ON THE WEB AT WWW.AMATOBOOKS.COM

Frank Amato Publications, Inc. • PO Box 82112 • Portland, Oregon 97282